# COMMUNICATION ENGLISH 1

SECOND EDITION

KMU CE Committee



Keimyung University Press

# Communication English 2nd Edition Book 1

KMU CE Committee



**Project Editor:** Casey Malarcher / **Acquisitions Editor:** Matthew Broadhurst / **Content Editor:** Peggy Anderson
**Illustrator:** Julia Filipone Erez / **Cover/Interior Design:** Design Plus

**ISBN:** 978-89-7585-806-2

11 10 9 8 7 6 5 4 3 2 1
21 20 19 18

**Photo Credits**
All images © Shutterstock, Inc.

Printed in Korea

# CONTENTS

# Map of the Book

| Unit | Title | Talking About |
|---|---|---|
| 01 | Introductions | Introducing ourselves to new people |
| 02 | Family | Members of our family |
| 03 | Sickness & Health | Being healthy and getting sick |
| 04 | Hobbies & Interests | What we like to do in our spare time |
| 05 | Holidays & Dates | Holidays, birthdays, and ordinal numbers |
| 06 | The Weather | Types of weather and the seasons |
| 07 | Food | Different types of food |
| 08 | Describing People | What people look like and how they act |
| 09 | Shopping | Going shopping |
| 10 | Movies & Television | Our favorite movies, TV programs, and actors |
| 11 | Telling Stories | Things that have happened to us |
| 12 | Travel | Travel and vacations |

# Classroom Language

| | | |
|---|---|---|
| 01 | Can I ask (you) a question? | 질문해도 될까요? |
| 02 | Could you repeat the instructions, please? | 어떻게 하는지 한 번 더 설명해주시겠어요? |
| 03 | What is our homework? | 숙제가 뭐예요? |
| 04 | How do you say that word? | 그 단어를 어떻게 말하나요? |
| 05 | How do you say "사전" in English? | "사전"을 영어로 어떻게 말하나요? |
| 06 | I don't know how to say it in English. | 영어로 어떻게 말하는지 모르겠어요. |
| 07 | I'm sorry Mr./Mrs./Miss/Ms. A, I didn't bring my English book. | A 선생님 죄송하지만, 영어책을 안 갖고 왔어요. |
| 08 | It's at home. | 집에 있습니다. |
| 09 | Did you have a good weekend? | 주말 잘 보냈나요? |
| 10 | I'm sorry I'm late. | 늦어서 죄송합니다. |
| 11 | When is this due? | 언제까지인가요? |
| 12 | Can I ask someone in Korean? | 한국어로 질문해도 될까요? |
| 13 | Do you mind if I speak Korean? | 한국어를 사용해도 될까요? |
| 14 | How do you spell "A"? | "A"의 철자는 무엇인가요? |
| 15 | We're finished. | 끝났습니다. |
| 16 | What do we do next? | 다음에는 무엇을 하나요? |
| 17 | Could I be excused? | 빠져도 될까요? / 화장실에 가도 될까요? |

# How to Use This Book

*Communication English* has been carefully structured to gradually introduce students to new topics, teaching them new vocabulary, grammar, and expressions until they are comfortable with speaking to a partner or to the class. Find out how each page works, and get ready to talk a lot!

## PAGE 1

**Warm-Up** uses a large photograph and simple activities to ease students into the new unit.

**Model Dialog** is a natural conversation designed to introduce the unit's vocabulary and grammar.

**Talking About** introduces students to the focus of the current unit.

**Speaking Success!** teaches elements of everyday spoken English to improve students' understanding and fluency.

## PAGE 2

**Vocabulary** introduces key vocabulary for the unit, and activities encourage students to use these words right away.

**Essential Expressions** features key vocabulary that will be useful in the rest of the unit.

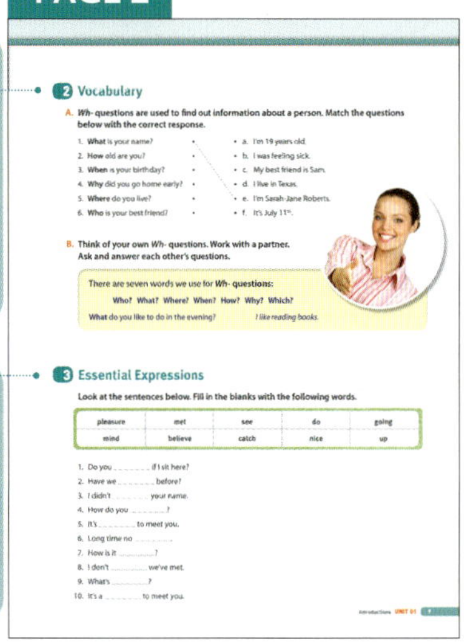


## PAGE 3

**Listening** features native speakers talking about themselves, allowing students to improve their listening comprehension skills.

To build fluency and confidence, example responses are provided with speaking activities.

## PAGE 4

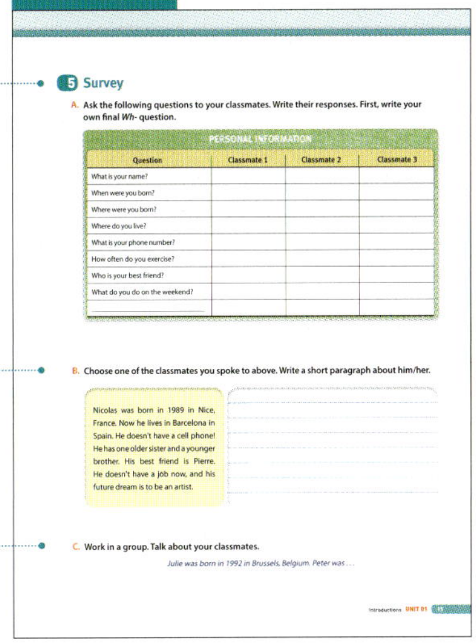


**Interview/Survey** sections introduce speaking more prominently, encouraging students to speak to other members of their class.

Students are asked to write down what they learn from speaking to their classmates.

Students are encouraged to work together to talk about what they have learned.

## PAGE 5

**Partner-Up** asks students to work with a partner in a range of speaking activities.

Working with a partner helps to improve students' speaking and confidence levels.

## PAGE 6

**Integrated Learning** concludes each unit, checking and expanding upon the skills learned throughout the unit.

More key skills are called upon, featuring reading and writing in addition to listening and speaking.

# UNIT 01 Introductions

Warm-Up

Say hello to your classmates.
Do you like to meet new people?

**Talking About:**
Introducing ourselves to new people

## 1 Model Dialog

**Listen and practice the dialog with a partner.** Track 1

**Simon:** Hello, I'm Simon. It's nice to meet you.

**Rachel:** Hi, Simon. My name is Rachel. Glad to meet you. Where are you from?

**Simon:** I'm from Montreal, Canada. I'm here to study history. What about you, Rachel?

**Rachel:** I'm from Canberra, Australia. I study English literature.

**Simon:** That's interesting. When did you come here?

**Rachel:** Two years ago. How about you, Simon?

**Simon:** I came here last month. Do you have any brothers or sisters?

**Rachel:** Yes, I have one sister. She lives with my parents.

**Simon:** I have a sister, too. Oh, my class is about to start! See you later.

**Rachel:** It was nice meeting you, Simon. Have a nice day!

### Speaking Success!

Auxiliary verbs are often **contracted** in everyday speech.

I am = **I'm**

That is = **That's**

You are = **You're**

We will = **We'll**

## 2 Vocabulary

**A.** ***Wh-*** **questions are used to find out information about a person. Match the questions below with the correct response.**

| | |
|---|---|
| 1. **What** is your name? • | • a. I'm 19 years old. |
| 2. **How** old are you? • | • b. I was feeling sick. |
| 3. **When** is your birthday? • | • c. My best friend is Sam. |
| 4. **Why** did you go home early? • | • d. I live in Texas. |
| 5. **Where** do you live? • | • e. I'm Sarah-Jane Roberts. |
| 6. **Who** is your best friend? • | • f. It's July 11th. |

**B. Think of your own** ***Wh-*** **questions. Work with a partner. Ask and answer each other's questions.**

> There are seven words we use for ***Wh-*** **questions:**
>
> **Who? What? Where? When? How? Why? Which?**
>
> **What** do you like to do in the evening? *I like reading books.*

## 3 Essential Expressions

**Look at the sentences below. Fill in the blanks with the following words.**

| pleasure | met | see | do | going |
|---|---|---|---|---|
| ~~mind~~ | believe | catch | nice | up |

1. Do you ___mind___ if I sit here?
2. Have we _________ before?
3. I didn't _________ your name.
4. How do you _________?
5. It's _________ to meet you.
6. Long time no _________.
7. How is it _________?
8. I don't _________ we've met.
9. What's _________?
10. It's a _________ to meet you.

## 4 Listening

**A.** **Look at the picture. This is Mary. What does she do? Discuss with a partner.**

**B.** **Listen to Mary being interviewed. Complete the sentences with her responses.** Track 2

1. My __name__ is __Mary__ hart.
2. I'm from __________, Canada.
3. I came to teach __________.
4. I've been here for almost __________ years.
5. I really __________ Spanish food!
6. Well, I love __________, and I like __________ __________, too.
7. Someday I'd like to open up my own __________.

**C.** **Listen again. Write a number next to each question in the order it is asked.**

____ Why did you come to Spain?

____ Where are you from?

____ What do you like best about Spain?

____ What do you do in your free time?

____ What's your dream for the future?

__1__ What is your name?

**D.** **Work with a partner. Take it in turns to describe Mary.**

*Mary Hart is from Vancouver, Canada.*
*She lives in Spain with her husband . . .*

## 5 Survey

A. Ask the following questions to your classmates. Write their responses. First, write your own final *Wh-* question.

PERSONAL INFORMATION

| Question | Classmate 1 | Classmate 2 | Classmate 3 |
|---|---|---|---|
| What is your name? | | | |
| When were you born? | | | |
| Where were you born? | | | |
| Where do you live? | | | |
| What is your phone number? | | | |
| How often do you exercise? | | | |
| Who is your best friend? | | | |
| What do you do on the weekend? | | | |
| ______________________ | | | |

B. Choose one of the classmates you spoke to above. Write a short paragraph about him/her.

Nicolas was born in 1989 in Nice, France. Now he lives in Barcelona in Spain. He doesn't have a cell phone! He has one older sister and a younger brother. His best friend is Pierre. He doesn't have a job now, and his future dream is to be an artist.

C. Work in a group. Talk about your classmates.

*Julie was born in 1992 in Brussels, Belgium. Peter was . . .*

## 6 Partner-Up

**A. Listen to the dialog and perform both roles with a partner.** Track 3

**Interviewer:** Hi, please sit down.

**Interviewee:** Hello, pleased to meet you.

**Interviewer:** So, could you tell me a little about yourself?

**Interviewee:** Yes, of course. My name is **Jack Malden**. I'm **21** years old and I live in **New York**.

**Interviewer:** OK, **Jack**. Why do you think you are the best person for this job?

**Interviewee:** Well, I am **hard-working** and **motivated**.

**Interviewer:** Do you have any work experience?

**Interviewee:** Yes, I was a **delivery boy** for **Pizza Party** for **two years**.

**Interviewer:** Very good. Thank you, **Jack**. We will be in touch.

**Interviewee:** Thank you. Goodbye!

**B. With your partner, practice the dialog with the following details.**

- Rahul Malik
- 18
- Cairo
- creative, open-minded
- cashier, Super Store, six months

- Susan Petrova
- 25
- St. Petersburg
- energetic, friendly
- waitress, La Padella, one year

- Mike Jones
- 17
- Manchester
- smart, punctual
- paperboy, News Time, four years

# Integrated Learning

## 1 Comprehension

**A. Work in a group. Read the passage below. Take turns reading it aloud.**

Dear Martin,

Hello! My name is Jake. It's nice to meet you! I have never had a pen-pal before. I hope that we will be friends for a long time! I guess you want to know about me, right? Well, I am from England. My birthday is on November 5$^{th}$ and I am 19 years old. I love playing computer games, and my favorite food is mince pie! Mince pie is a special dessert made from fruits and spices. Have you ever tried it? Please write back. I want to know all about you, and about France!

Your new friend,
***Jake Verne***

**B. Read Jake's letter again. Answer the questions. Try to use full sentences.**

1. Who wrote this letter? Jake Verne wrote this letter.
2. Where does Martin come from? ______
3. What does Jake like to do? ______
4. Has Jake had a pen-pal before? ______
5. What is mince pie made from? ______
6. What does Jake hope? ______
7. When is Jake's birthday? ______

**C. Role-Play: Pretend you are a different person, from a different country. A partner will interview you. Tell him/her all about yourself and your new country!**

*My name is Miguel. I am from Mexico. I like riding horses and playing the guitar.*

*My name is Christian. I am from Norway. I like riding my bike.*

# Practice

## 1 Dialog

**A. Listen to the recording and put the missing words into the dialog.** Track 1

| meeting | lives | glad | month |
|---|---|---|---|
| meet | sisters | ago | history |

**Simon:** Hello, I'm Simon. It's nice to ________ you.

**Rachel:** Hi, Simon. My name is Rachel. ________ to meet you. Where are you from?

**Simon:** I'm from **Montreal**, **Canada**. I'm here to study ________. What about you, Rachel?

**Rachel:** I'm from **Canberra**, **Australia**. I study **English literature**.

**Simon:** That's interesting. When did you come here?

**Rachel:** **Two** years ________. How about you, Simon?

**Simon:** I came here last ________. Do you have any brothers or ___________?

**Rachel:** Yes, I have one sister. She ________ with my parents.

**Simon:** I have a sister, too. Oh, my class is about to start! See you later.

**Rachel:** It was nice ________________ you, Simon. Have a nice day!

**B. Look at the bolded words in the dialog above. With a partner, think of some new information to replace these words.**

**C. Practice the dialog using the new information.**

## 2 Picture Description

**Listen and choose the statement that best describes what you see in the picture.** Track 4

1. 

Ⓐ Ⓑ Ⓒ Ⓓ

2. 

Ⓐ Ⓑ Ⓒ Ⓓ

## 3 Unscramble

**Unscramble the sentences below.**

1. drove here, / I / traffic jam. / there was / and / a huge
   → I drove here, and there was a huge traffic jam.

2. wanted to / visit you, / He / but / recently. / he's so busy
   → ______________________________

3. won the / Last year, / I / prize / best newcomer. / for
   → ______________________________

4. had couscous / which I / I / really / for lunch, / like.
   → ______________________________

5. reading books / Andrea likes / mostly crime / in the evening, / novels.
   → ______________________________

# Note Taking

| Main Points | Detail |
| --- | --- |
| | |
| | |
| | |
| | |
| | |
| | |

| Summary |
| --- |
| |
| |
| |
| |
| |
| |

# Brainstorming

# Journal/Activity Writing

# UNIT 02 Family

**Warm-Up**

How many people are in your family?
Do you have any brothers or sisters? Who do you like best?

**Talking About:**
Members of our family

## 1 Model Dialog

**Listen and practice the dialog with a partner.** Track 5

**Rasheed:** My sister is getting married next week.

**Jen:** Wow, that's great! I don't have any siblings.

**Rasheed:** Oh, really? I have two sisters and a brother.

**Jen:** That's a lot! How old are they?

**Rasheed:** Hmm . . . let me think. My younger sister is 6, and my older sister is 26.

**Jen:** What about your brother? How old is he?

**Rasheed:** He's, uh . . . 18. We're good friends. We often play soccer together.

**Jen:** That sounds nice. I'm an only child.

**Rasheed:** Is it boring at home? My brother is my best friend.

**Jen:** Not at all. My dad comes home early to play video games with me.

### Speaking Success!

When speaking, we often use **vocalized pauses** as we think of what to say. These are not used in written English.

**Uh . . .**

**Umm . . .**

**Hmm . . .**

## 2 Vocabulary

**A.** **Listen to these words for family members. Repeat the words after the recording.** Track 6

brother son husband grandfather nephew father uncle

| | |
|---|---|
| wife | |
| mother | |
| daughter | |
| aunt | |
| grandmother | |
| niece | |
| sister | |

**B.** **Use these words to complete the pairs in the chart above.**

**C.** **Work with a partner. Make sentences about your family. Use the vocabulary words above.**

*My **grandmother** is very friendly.* *I don't have a **wife**.*

## 3 Essential Expressions

**Look at the sentences below. Fill in the blanks with the following words.**

| niece | brother | daughter |
|---|---|---|
| wife | grandfather | uncle |

1. My twin ________________ is twenty minutes older than me.
2. I love to hear my ________________'s stories of what the world was like sixty years ago.
3. I go fishing with my ________________ and his two sons every summer.
4. My ________________ is two years old and she is just so adorable!
5. Colin and his ________________ are going to Paris for their wedding anniversary.
6. She is the ________________ of my mother's sister—so she is my cousin!

## 4 Listening

**A.** **Look at the pictures. Which of these women do you think is married? Who has children?**

**B.** **Listen to these women answer some questions about their families. Write their responses below.** Track 7

**Nina**

1. How old is Christina? ______
2. How old is Tony? ______

**Stephanie**

3. How many brothers or sisters does Stephanie have? ______________
4. What are their names? ______________________________

**Hilda**

5. How old are Hilda's children?

 a. Ron ______
 b. Marilyn ______
 c. Eric ______
 d. Steven ______
 e. Janet ______

**C.** **Listen again. Fill in the chart.**

| | Is she married? | Does she have any brothers? | How many? | Does she have any sisters? | How many? |
|---|---|---|---|---|---|
| Nina | | | | | |
| Stephanie | | | | | |
| Hilda | | | | | |

**D.** **Work with a partner. Ask and answer questions about these women. Use *"Who . . . ?"***

Who has three older brothers? *That's Stephanie.*

Who has a sister called Christina? *Nina does.*

## 5 Interview

**A. Work with a partner. Ask the following questions about his/her family. Write down the answers.**

1. Do you have any brothers or sisters?

2. How old are your brothers and sisters?

3. How old are your parents?

4. Where are your parents from?

5. Are your parents strict?

6. How often do you visit your grandparents?

7. Where do your cousins live?

8. Do you look like your mom?

9. Can your dad cook?

10. How old are your grandparents?

**B. Work in a group. Talk about the person you spoke to above.**

*Steve doesn't have any brothers or sisters. He doesn't know how old his parents are! His mom is Korean and his dad is from Canada . . .*

**C. As a class, ask your teacher the above questions. Think of some more questions to ask.**

*Are you married? Do you have any children?*

## 6 Partner-Up

**A. Let's play a game! Play with a partner. Follow the steps below to play Blackout.**

- Choose nine of the vocabulary words below and write them in the grid. Use a pencil so you can play again!
- Choose a word, and then give a hint to help your partner guess it. Remember: don't say the word! Keep giving clues until your partner guesses correctly.
- Cross out the word. If your partner has the same word, he/she can cross it out, too.
- The person who wins is the first person to cross out all his/her words and say, "Blackout!"

**Vocab note**

An **in-law** is someone who is related to you by marriage.

brother-in-law niece cousin mother sister-in-law nephew grandmother
parents mother-in-law uncle grandfather father-in-law aunt father

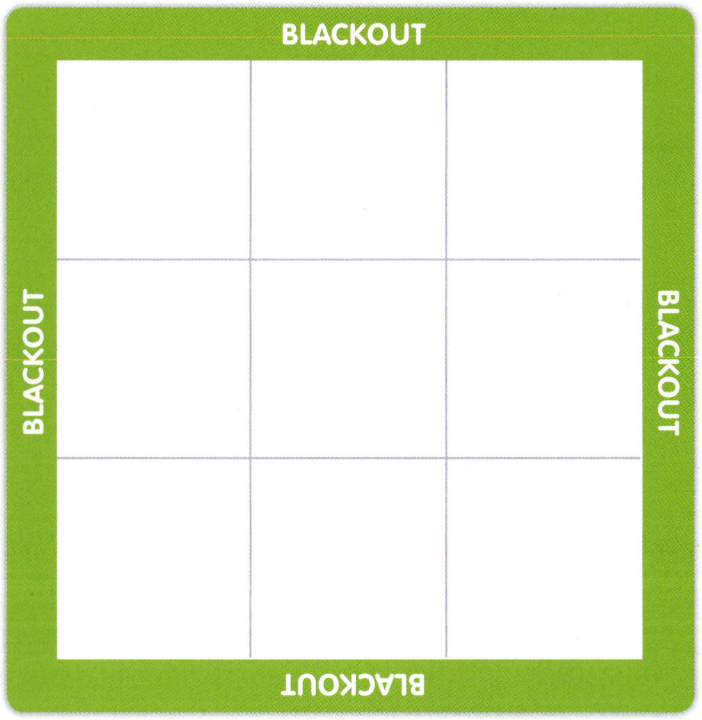


**B. Work in a group. Talk about a member of your own family.**

*My brother-in-law is called Freddy. He's 32 years old. He's my sister's husband. He's really tall and very funny, and we're good friends.*

# Integrated Learning

## 1 Comprehension

**A. Listen to Joe talk about his relatives and fill in the chart.** Track 8

| | Relation | Age | City | Is he/she married? | Does he/she have children? | Does he/she have a job? |
|---|---|---|---|---|---|---|
| A. Robert | | | | | | |
| B. Jack | | | | | | |
| C. Laurie | | | | | | |
| D. Rosie | | | | | | |
| E. Darren | | | | | | |

**B. Listen again to the correct answers. Check with a partner.**

*You said Laurie is 53 years old. Actually, she is 43.*

**C. Look at the family tree below and answer the questions with the correct names.**

1. Who are Cindy's parents?
____________________
2. Who is Albert's uncle?
____________________
3. Who is Wilma's son?
____________________
4. Who is Cindy's cousin?
____________________
5. Who is Ed's brother-in-law?
____________________
6. Who is Dan's grandmother?
____________________

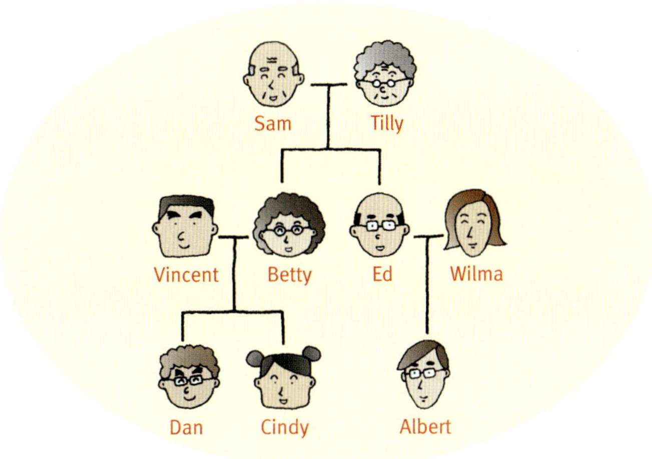


**D. Using this family tree for help, make your own family tree on a piece of paper. Discuss it with your partner.**

*This is my father. He has two brothers. His parents are called . . .*

# Practice

## 1 Dialog

**A. Listen to the recording and put the missing words into the dialog.** Track 5

| any | married | together | younger |
|---|---|---|---|
| sounds | boring | early | have |

| | |
|---|---|
| Rasheed: | My **sister** is getting ________ next week. |
| Jen: | Wow, that's great! I don't have ________ siblings. |
| Rasheed: | Oh, really? I ________ two sisters and a brother. |
| Jen: | That's a lot! How old are they? |
| Rasheed: | Hmm . . . let me think. My ________ sister is **6**, and my older sister is **26**. |
| Jen: | What about your brother? How old is he? |
| Rasheed: | He's, uh . . . **18**. We are good friends. We often play **soccer** ____________. |
| Jen: | That ________ nice. I'm an only child. |
| Rasheed: | Is it ________ at home? My brother is my best friend. |
| Jen: | Not at all. My dad comes home ________ to **play video games** with me. |

**B. Look at the bolded words in the dialog above. With a partner, think of some new information to replace these words.**

**C. Practice the dialog using the new information.**

## 2 Picture Description

**Listen and choose the statement that best describes what you see in the picture.** Track 9

1.

Ⓐ Ⓑ Ⓒ Ⓓ

2.

Ⓐ Ⓑ Ⓒ Ⓓ

## 3 Unscramble

**Unscramble the sentences below.**

1. are not / to make it / We / going to be / tonight. / able
→ ______________________________

2. thesis / writing my / right now. / I am
→ ______________________________

3. dog is / chasing / Our / tail. / own / his
→ ______________________________

4. happy to / We are / son. / see you,
→ ______________________________

5. Terry / going to / is / late for / be / own party! / his
→ ______________________________

# Note Taking

| Main Points | Detail |
|---|---|
| | |
| | |
| | |
| | |
| | |
| | |

| Summary |
|---|
| |
| |
| |
| |
| |
| |

# Brainstorming

# Journal/Activity Writing

# UNIT 03 Sickness & Health

Warm-Up

Do you think that you are healthy?
Do you exercise often?

**Talking About:**
Being healthy and getting sick

## 1 Model Dialog

**Listen and practice the dialog with a partner.** Track 10

| | |
|---|---|
| Ellie: | Trevor, how are you doing? I haven't seen you for a while. |
| Trevor: | Hey, Ellie. Yeah, I've been really sick for the last few days. |
| Ellie: | Oh, no, are you OK? I heard there was a virus going around. My mom was sick. |
| Trevor: | I guess I had that. I had a headache, a runny nose, and a bad stomach. |
| Ellie: | Oh, that's horrible. Are you feeling better now? |
| Trevor: | A little bit. I have an exam today, so I had to come in. |
| Ellie: | If you feel really sick, just tell your teacher. I'm sure she'll understand. |
| Trevor: | She won't. My teacher is Miss Anderton. She hates sick people. |
| Ellie: | I know her. She's super-fit, isn't she? She exercises every day. |
| Trevor: | And she's never sick. She'll say it's my fault! It's so unfair! |

### Speaking Success!

There are a few ways that we can talk about **non-specific periods of time.**

**A few days** = *three or more days*

**A couple (of) days** = *two days*

**A moment** = *a brief amount of time*

**A while** = *a longer period of time*

## 2 Vocabulary

**Work with a partner. Write the number of each body part next to its name.**

face ____
forehead ____
eyebrow ____
eyelashes ____
eye ____
nose ____
ear ____
cheek ____
mouth ____
lip ____
tooth ____
chin ____
neck ____
arm ____
shoulder ____
armpit ____

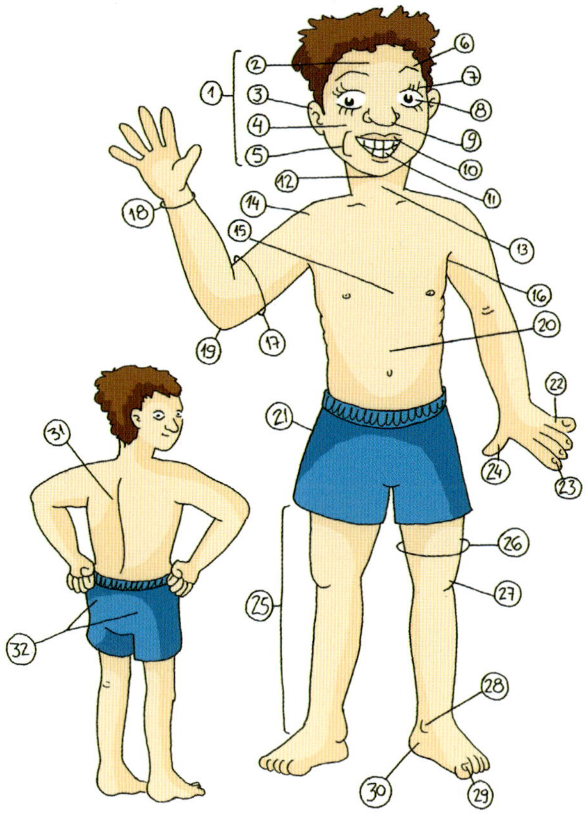


____ chest
____ elbow
____ wrist
____ finger
____ fingernail
____ thumb
____ stomach
____ hips
____ back
____ bottom
____ leg
____ thigh
____ knee
____ ankle
____ heel
____ toe

## 3 Essential Expressions

**Look at the sentences below. Fill in the blanks with the following words.**

| stomachache | fever | nose |
|---|---|---|
| allergy | sore | toothache |

1. I went to the dentist this week because I had a bad ____________.
2. I don't like summer since I have a bad pollen ____________.
3. My mom made me a honey and lemon drink for my ____________ throat.
4. The ____________ kept him in bed for a whole week.
5. She had a bad cold that week, and could hardly breathe out of her ____________.
6. He thinks that he might have gotten the ____________ from some bad sushi he ate.

## 4 Listening

**A. Listen to Dean talking about his habits. Write a number next to each question in the order it is asked.** Track 11

a. Do you have your teeth cleaned once a year? _____
b. Do you exercise at least three times a week? _____
c. Do you catch a cold more than twice a year? _____
d. Do you usually get enough sleep? _____
e. Do you eat fruits and vegetables almost every day? _____
f. Do you smoke more than three cigarettes a day? _____
g. Is work or school stressful for you? _____
h. Do you get drunk once or more per month? _____
i. Do you need to lose weight? _____
j. Do you eat junk food almost every day? _____

**B. Listen again to the questions in the correct order. Does Dean answer "Yes" or "No" to these questions? Circle "Yes" or "No" below.**

1. Yes No
2. Yes No
3. Yes No
4. Yes No
5. Yes No
6. Yes No
7. Yes No
8. Yes No
9. Yes No
10. Yes No

**Scoring**

| Question | Points Yes | Points No | Question | Points Yes | Points No |
|---|---|---|---|---|---|
| 1 | −3 | +3 | 6 | −1 | +1 |
| 2 | +3 | −3 | 7 | +1 | −1 |
| 3 | −2 | +2 | 8 | +3 | −3 |
| 4 | +2 | −2 | 9 | −2 | +2 |
| 5 | −2 | +2 | 10 | −3 | +3 |

| Points | |
|---|---|
| 10 to 20 | Excellent health |
| 0 to 9 | Healthy |
| −1 to −9 | Unhealthy |
| −10 to −20 | Very unhealthy |

**C. Look at the points system above, and Dean's answers from Activity B. Work out how many points he gets. How healthy is Dean?**

**D. Work with a partner. Ask and answer questions that Dean is asked. Look at your score. How healthy are you?**

*I don't smoke at all, and I don't drink alcohol. I . . .*

## 5 Survey

**A. Work with a partner. Talk about and match each symptom to the related illness.**

1. My throat hurts when I swallow. •
2. My eyes itch and I sneeze a lot. •
3. My ear hurts. •
4. My stomach hurts. •
5. My head aches. •
6. My back hurts. •
7. I feel very hot. •
8. My tooth hurts. •

• a. a stomachache
• b. a headache
• c. a backache
• d. an allergy
• e. an earache
• f. a fever
• g. a sore throat
• h. a toothache

**B. Find two classmates. Ask the following questions. Write their responses.**

| | NAME ________ | NAME ________ |
|---|---|---|
| How good is your eyesight? | | |
| When was the last time you threw up? | | |
| How often do you get a headache? | | |
| Do you have any allergies? | | |
| Do you ever get motion sickness? | | |
| What's the highest temperature you've ever had? | | |
| What's something that makes you feel dizzy? | | |
| What's something that makes you feel nauseous? | | |
| Have you ever been in the hospital? What for? | | |
| Have you ever broken a bone? How did it happen? | | |

**C. Work in a group. Discuss your answers to the questions.**

## 6 Partner-Up

**A.** **Work with a partner. Look at the crossword below. One of you is partner A, and the other is Partner B. Cover up your partner's clues. Give each other clues and attempt to complete the crossword.**

### Partner A

**Down hints**

1. Feeling as if you might throw up.
3. The upper part of your leg.
6. When you are sick, this will be high.
7. A hole in your tooth.
8. A reflex action that causes quick short breaths.

### Partner B

**Across hints**

2. You are sneezing, and you have itchy, watery eyes.
4. The world feels like it is spinning.
5. It hurts when you swallow.
8. You have a pain in your head.
9. Your body aches and you have a fever, you are very tired.
10. To push air from the lungs suddenly and with a loud noise.
11. If these hurt, you may have trouble hearing.

How do you spell it?

**B.** **Work in a group. Compare your answers.**

**C.** **Your teacher will give you the correct answers. How many did you get correct?**

# Integrated Learning

## 1 Comprehension

**A. Listen to Hayley talk about the health problems that she has experienced. Write down her answers to these questions.** Track 12

1. How often does she get a cold? ______________________
2. How often does she get a headache? ______________________
3. When was the last time she had the flu? ______________________
4. Does she have any allergies? ______________________
5. Why was she in the hospital? ______________________
6. What's something that makes her feel nauseous? ______________________
7. What's something that makes her feel dizzy? ______________________

**B. Work in a group. Discuss Hayley's health, and compare it to your own.**

*I think Hayley is reasonably healthy. She seems to have had many illnesses, but . . .*

**C. Let's play a game! Play in a group.**

- Silently act out an illness or health condition. No speaking!
- Your teammates will try to guess the illness.
- Whoever guesses correctly acts out next.
- Use other illness words from this unit when you have finished those on this page.

· cough · hiccups
· sneeze · sunburn
· throw up · cavity

# Practice

## 1 Dialog

**A. Listen to the recording and put the missing words into the dialog.** Track 10

| better | understand | doing | while |
|---|---|---|---|
| exercises | never | really | guess |

**Ellie:** Trevor, how are you ____________? I haven't seen you for a ________.

**Trevor:** Hey, Ellie. Yeah, I've been ________ sick for the last few days.

**Ellie:** Oh, no, are you OK? I heard there was a virus going around. My mom was sick.

**Trevor:** I ________ I had that. I had a **headache**, runny nose, and a **bad stomach**.

**Ellie:** Oh, that's horrible. Are you feeling __________ now?

**Trevor:** A little bit. I have an exam **today**, so I had to come in.

**Ellie:** If you feel really sick, just tell your teacher. I'm sure she'll ______________.

**Trevor:** She won't. My teacher is **Miss Anderton**. She hates sick people.

**Ellie:** I know her. She's super-fit, isn't she? She ____________ every day.

**Trevor:** And she's ___________ sick. She'll say it's my fault! It's so **unfair**!

**B. Look at the bolded words in the dialog above. With a partner, think of some new information to replace these words.**

**C. Practice the dialog using the new information.**

## 2 Picture Description

**Listen and choose the statement that best describes what you see in the picture.** Track 13

**1.**

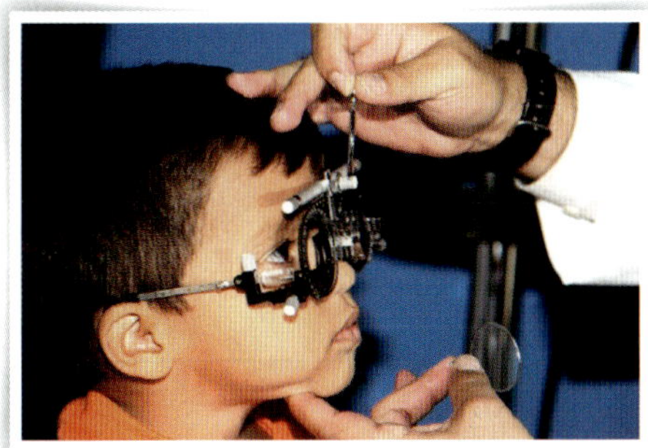

Ⓐ Ⓑ Ⓒ Ⓓ

**2.**

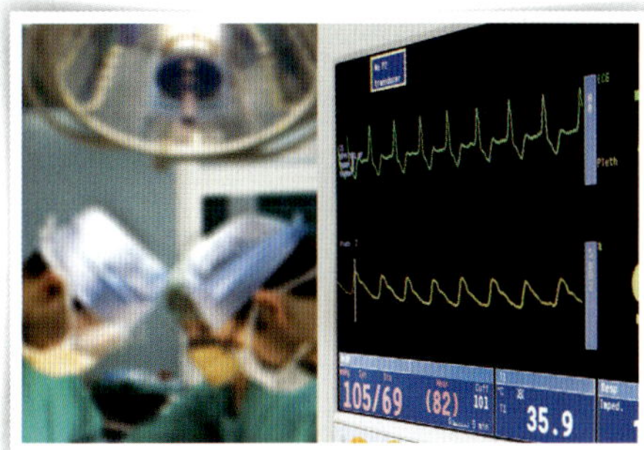


Ⓐ Ⓑ Ⓒ Ⓓ

## 3 Unscramble

**Unscramble the sentences below.**

1. was young, / When I / got / really bad / I / headaches.
   → ______________________________

2. allergies? / have / you / any / Do
   → ______________________________

3. ever / Have you / hospital? / go to / had to / the
   → ______________________________

4. hours of / How many / sleep / usually get? / do you
   → ______________________________

5. bad / I / back. / a / have
   → ______________________________

# Note Taking

| Main Points | Detail |
|---|---|
| | |
| | |
| | |
| | |
| | |
| | |

| Summary |
|---|
| |
| |
| |
| |
| |
| |

# Brainstorming

# Journal/Activity Writing

# UNIT 04 Hobbies & Interests

Warm-Up

What do you do when you get home after class?
What is something that you are really good at?

**Talking About:**
What we like to do in our spare time

## 1 Model Dialog

**Listen and practice the dialog with a partner.** Track 14

**Amy:** Daniel, are you busy this evening?
**Daniel:** Actually, I am. I'm going swimming with my friends.
**Amy:** Cool! Do you go swimming often?
**Daniel:** Uh-huh. I go at least twice a week. It's great exercise.
**Amy:** Oh, that's good. I'm not a very good swimmer. I'm not very athletic.
**Daniel:** What do you like to do in your spare time, then?
**Amy:** I like to stay at home and read a book or watch television.
**Daniel:** I love reading! I try to read every night before I go to sleep.
**Amy:** You do? We should go to the library together sometime.
**Daniel:** Sure, I'd like that. I have to go now. See you later!

### Speaking Success!

There are a number of ways that we can say "yes" in casual speech.

**Uh-huh.**
**Sure.**
**Yeah.**
**Yep.**

## 2 Vocabulary

**Complete the sentences with the correct action verb.**

play surf paint drive speak sing eat cook

1. I love to go to the beach and ______________ the waves.
2. I can ______________ the piano.
3. I like ______________ing to myself.
4. Andy ______________ed a picture on the weekend.
5. Can you ______________ Italian?
6. I can ______________ pasta, but not much else.
7. I want to ______________ my car this weekend.
8. I love to ______________ cold pizza for breakfast.

## 3 Essential Expressions

**Look at the sentences below. Fill in the blanks with the following words.**

| sing | paint | speaking | eat |
|---|---|---|---|
| cook | surfing | play | drive |

1. I'm going to go ______________ with my cousin who lives by the beach.
2. I like to ______________ dinner for my girlfriend.
3. In his spare time, Jake likes to ______________ landscapes.
4. If I had a car, I would ______________ it everywhere!
5. Jane loves to ______________ in the shower.
6. Charles and Barry like to ______________ soccer on Sundays.
7. I like ______________ to my relatives over the webcam.
8. I like to ______________ at new restaurants and take pictures of the food.

## 4 Listening

**A.** Listen to David being interviewed. Fill in the boxes below. Some activities can fit in more than one box. Track 15

| David likes . . . | David doesn't like . . . |
|---|---|
| | |

| David can . . . | David can't . . . |
|---|---|
| | |

**B.** Why doesn't David like these activities? Listen again and write his reasons.

1. baseball ____________________
2. karate ____________________
3. soccer ____________________
4. football ____________________
5. swimming ____________________

**C.** Work with a partner. Speak about David's likes and dislikes, and what he can and cannot do.

*David likes playing basketball the most. He . . .*

**D.** Think about yourself. What are five things you like and five things you dislike? What about five things you can and cannot do?

*I like drawing comics. I can't drive a car . . .*

## 5 Survey

A. Ask the following questions to your classmates. Write their names in the chart below. Try to find three people who answer "yes" to each question.

**Who . . . ?**

| | Name | Name | Name |
|---|---|---|---|
| . . . can drive well | | | |
| . . . doesn't like doing dishes | | | |
| . . . can play a musical instrument | | | |
| . . . likes gardening | | | |
| . . . doesn't like spicy foods | | | |
| . . . can say "hello" in four languages | | | |
| . . . doesn't like to watch television | | | |
| . . . likes to send text messages | | | |
| . . . can dance really well | | | |
| . . . loves Italian food | | | |
| . . . loves computer games | | | |
| . . . doesn't like coffee | | | |

B. Choose one person you spoke to above. Ask for more details about his/her answers.

*Tanya doesn't like to watch television.*
*She likes going to the movies, however.*

C. Complete the three questions below, and then ask your teacher.

1. Do you like ______________________________
2. Can you ______________________________
3. Are you good at ______________________________

## 6 Partner-Up

**A.** **Work with different partners. Ask the following questions about favorites. Before you begin, write you own final two questions.**

**What's your favorite . . .**

| | You | Name ________ | Name ________ | Name ________ |
|---|---|---|---|---|
| . . . color? | | | | |
| . . . sport? | | | | |
| . . . kind of food? | | | | |
| . . . zoo animal? | | | | |
| . . . video game? | | | | |
| . . . fast food? | | | | |
| . . . day of the week? | | | | |
| . . . flavor of ice cream? | | | | |
| . . . television program? | | | | |
| . . . genre of music? | | | | |
| . . . movie? | | | | |
| . . . actor's/actress's name? | | | | |
| . . . comedian's name? | | | | |
| ________ | | | | |
| ________ | | | | |

**B.** **Work in a group. Take turns talking about another group member, but don't say the person's name! Give clues to your group to help them guess who you are talking about.**

*This person's favorite food is spaghetti, and their favorite actor is Brad Pitt . . .*

**C.** **Ask a partner the same questions, changing "favorite" to "least favorite."**

What's your least favorite flavor of ice cream? *Strawberry. It's just too sweet for me.*

# Integrated Learning

## 1 Comprehension

**A.** Listen to Kenta, Jackie, Matt, and Tina talk about their likes and dislikes. Fill in the chart as you listen. Track 16

| | Loves | Likes | Doesn't like | Hates |
|---|---|---|---|---|
| 1. Kenta | | | | |
| 2. Jackie | | | | |
| 3. Matt | | | | |
| 4. Tina | | | | |

**B.** What do you love? What do you hate? Discuss with a partner.

*I love watching TV and eating pizza at the same time! I hate feeling sick on the weekend.*

**C.** Read the passage below out loud. Write about your own favorite hobby.

I love playing computer games. I know it's not cool, but I really like it. When I was in elementary school, I came home one day, and my dad had bought me a second-hand video game console. It was quite old already, but it came with a lot of games. I ran home every day to play it! Dad and I played together on weekends. I still play it sometimes when I get bored.

**D.** Walk around the class and look for people who share your interests.

# Practice

## 1 Dialog

**A. Listen to the recording and put the missing words into the dialog.** Track 14

| stay | often | sometime | evening |
|---|---|---|---|
| spare | busy | friends | should |

**Amy:** Daniel, are you ________ this ________________?

**Daniel:** Actually, I am. I'm going **swimming** with my _______________.

**Amy:** Cool! Do you go **swimming** ___________?

**Daniel:** Uh-huh. I go at least **twice** a week. It's great exercise.

**Amy:** Oh, that's good. I'm not a very good **swimmer**. I'm not very athletic.

**Daniel:** What do you like to do in your ________ time, then?

**Amy:** I like to ________ at home and read a book or **watch television**.

**Daniel:** I love reading! I try to read every night before I go to sleep.

**Amy:** You do? We ____________ go to the library together _______________.

**Daniel:** Sure, I'd like that. I have to go now. See you later!

**B. Look at the bolded words in the dialog above. With a partner, think of some new information to replace these words.**

**C. Practice the dialog using the new information.**

## 2 Picture Description

**Listen and choose the statement that best describes what you see in the picture.** Track 17

1.

Ⓐ Ⓑ Ⓒ Ⓓ

2.

Ⓐ Ⓑ Ⓒ Ⓓ

## 3 Unscramble

**Unscramble the sentences below.**

1. cannot sing / very well / I / at all.
   → ______________________________

2. and Greg / really like / Tom / the sauna. / going to
   → ______________________________

3. She / play the / really well. / can / piano
   → ______________________________

4. doesn't like / Paul / waking / early. / up
   → ______________________________

5. be by / I / like to / weekends. / myself / on the
   → ______________________________

# Note Taking

| Main Points | Detail |
| --- | --- |
| | |
| | |
| | |
| | |
| | |
| | |

| Summary |
| --- |
| |
| |
| |
| |
| |
| |

# Brainstorming

# Journal/Activity Writing

# UNIT 05 Holidays & Dates

**Warm-Up**

What is your favorite holiday?
What did you do for your last birthday?

**Talking About:**
Holidays, birthdays, and ordinal numbers

## 1 Model Dialog

**Listen and practice the dialog with a partner.** Track 18

**Betty:** Happy birthday, Michael! It's not much, but I got you this card.
**Michael:** Wow . . . thanks. Actually, it's not my birthday today.
**Betty:** It's not? Oh, no! How did I get that wrong?
**Michael:** It's OK. My birthday is next month, the 14th.
**Betty:** February 14th? Your birthday is on Valentine's Day?
**Michael:** Yeah, it is. It's a little embarrassing, to be honest.
**Betty:** Why's that? I love Valentine's Day! It's my absolute favorite holiday.
**Michael:** Well, my mom always gets me a card with roses on it.
**Betty:** That's funny. She sounds like fun. Well, do you want this card or not?
**Michael:** Yeah, I suppose so. It's better than roses again! Thanks, Betty.

### Speaking Success!

Questions which are not intended to be answered are called **rhetorical questions.**

**How did I get that wrong?**
**Is the sky blue?**
**It would be, wouldn't it?**
**Will he save the day?**

## 2 Vocabulary

**A.** **Write the correct ordinal number next to its cardinal equivalent.**

twelfth    twenty-third    first    forty-second    fourth    two hundredth    ninth

1. **1** ______________
2. **12** ______________
3. **23** ______________
4. **4** ______________
5. **42** ______________
6. **9** ______________
7. **200** ______________

Cardinal numbers are regular numbers, used for counting.

***One** apple*    ***Eleven** soccer players*

Ordinal numbers are used to put numbers in order.

*I won **first** prize!*    *It's the **second** time this week.*

## 3 Essential Expressions

**Look at the sentences below. Fill in the blanks with the following words.**

| 200th | 23rd | first | 12th |
|---|---|---|---|
| fourth | ninth | 42nd | |

1. Today is my ______________ birthday. Next year, I'll be a teenager.
2. This year marks the ______________ anniversary of the birth of their nation.
3. Joy won ______________ prize in the science contest, but only the top three winners get a medal.
4. She came in ______________ in the talent competition, just ahead of the tenth place.
5. Mike's birthday is on the ______________ of this month. Mine is one week earlier on the 16th.
6. Jeff is nervous because this is his ______________ trip on an airplane.
7. The family will be having a party for Gary's mother's ______________ birthday.

# 4 Listening

**A.** **Work with a partner. Look at this chart of Western holidays. Fill in the blanks with the dates and holidays below.**

**Dates**

- January $1^{st}$
- July $1^{st}$
- January $26^{th}$
- July $4^{th}$
- February $14^{th}$
- October $31^{st}$
- April $1^{st}$
- November $11^{th}$
- April $23^{rd}$
- December $25^{th}$
- May $1^{st}$
- December $26^{th}$

| When | What | Where |
|---|---|---|
| January $1^{st}$ | New Year's Day | All four countries |
| 1) | Australia Day | Australia |
| 2) | Valentine's Day | All four countries |
| April $1^{st}$ | 3) | All four countries |
| 4) | St. George's Day | England, part of Canada |
| May $1^{st}$ | May Day | England, parts of the United States |
| 5) | Canada Day | Canada |
| July $4^{th}$ | 6) | United States |
| 7) | Halloween | All four countries |
| 8) | Remembrance/ Veterans Day | All four countries |
| December $25^{th}$ | 9) | All four countries |
| December $26^{th}$ | Boxing Day | Australia, Canada, England |

**Holidays**

- April Fools' Day
- Australia Day
- Boxing Day
- Canada Day
- Christmas
- Halloween
- Independence Day
- May Day
- New Year's Day
- Remembrance/ Veterans Day
- St. George's Day
- Valentine's Day

**B.** **Listen to the correct answers. Check with a partner.** Track 19

**C.** **Do you know anything about the holidays above? Work in a group. Discuss each holiday, giving as much information as you can.**

*On Valentine's Day, people give flowers and chocolates to the ones they love . . .*

**D.** **What are some public holidays in your country? Talk about them in your group.**

*Chuseok is similar to Thanksgiving in the USA. Our families gather and . . .*

## 5 Survey

**A.** Walk around your class. Ask the following questions to your classmates. Write their responses in the chart below.

| Name | When is your birthday? | What year were you born? | How old are you? |
|---|---|---|---|
| | | | |
| | | | |
| | | | |
| | | | |
| | | | |
| | | | |
| | | | |
| | | | |
| | | | |

**B.** Choose five classmates you spoke to above. Ask them about their birthdays. Think of your own questions.

What was the best present you ever received?
*A toy fire engine on my eighth birthday.*

What food do you like to eat on your birthday?
*I love any kind of cake!*

**C.** Work in a group. Discuss what you have learned about your classmates.

*Joan's birthday is March 15th.*
*She goes to the movies every year with her sister . . .*

## 6 Partner-Up

**A. Listen to the dialog and perform both roles with a partner.** Track 20

**Brad:** Hi, **Claire**. Are you excited for tomorrow?

**Claire:** Of course, **Brad**! It's **Christmas Day**! My favorite day of the year!

**Brad:** Me, too! What will you do?

**Claire:** I will **open presents with my family**.

**Brad:** Oh, that's great. What about food? Will you have a special meal?

**Claire:** Usually I **eat roast turkey** with my **close family**.

**Brad:** Sounds good! I love **Christmas Day** too. Do you know why?

**Claire:** No, why is that?

**Brad:** It's the day before my birthday!

**Claire:** So, your birthday is **December 26th**? I hope it's a good one!

**B. With your partner, practice the dialog with the following details.**

- Katie
- Marcus
- Thanksgiving
- visit my grandparents
- eat turkey, sweet potatoes and pumpkin pie
- whole family
- this Friday

- Amanda
- Richard
- Halloween
- go trick-or-treating with my best friend
- share my candy
- friends and brothers
- November 1st

- Bethany
- Jerry
- New Year's Eve
- have a party at my house
- just have a drink
- friends
- January 1st

**C. What is your favorite holiday? Work in a group. Talk about your favorite day of the year.**

*I love February 14th. It's Valentine's Day! My boyfriend usually buys . . .*

# Integrated Learning

## 1 Comprehension

**A.** **Read the passage below. Work with a partner. Take turns reading it aloud. Correct any pronunciation mistakes your partner makes.**

Dear Diary,

Yesterday was the best day of my life! It was July 11$^{th}$, my birthday. Because it was my 21$^{st}$ birthday, my parents got me a really special present. They bought me a car! It is only a second-hand car, but it is much better than driving mom's car everywhere! I really feel free now. My friends gave me a surprise birthday party, too! I was so happy, as it is the first time I have had a surprise party. I thought they had forgotten, but when I got home, all of my friends were in the living room! There must have been more than thirty people. We had a great time.

***Ellie***

**B.** **Read Ellie's diary entry again. Answer the questions. Use full sentences.**

1. What was yesterday's date? ______________________________
2. How old is Ellie? ______________________________
3. What did her friends do for her? ______________________________
4. What did her parents buy her? ______________________________
5. Where were Ellie's friends? ______________________________
6. How many friends surprised Ellie? ______________________________
7. Why does she feel free now? ______________________________

**C.** **When was your best birthday ever? Work in a group. Ask each other questions about your best birthday memories.**

When was your best birthday? — *It was 2003.*

Why was it so special? — *My friends took me to a concert.*

# Practice

## 1 Dialog

**A. Listen to the recording and put the missing words into the dialog.** Track 18

| embarrassing | actually | birthday | funny |
|---|---|---|---|
| suppose | much | better | absolute |

Betty: Happy birthday, Michael! It's not ________, but I got you this card.

Michael: Wow . . . thanks. __________, it's not my birthday today.

Betty: It's not? Oh, no! How did I get that wrong?

Michael: It's OK. My birthday is next month, the **14th**.

Betty: **February 14th**? Your ________________ is on **Valentine's Day**?

Michael: Yeah, it is. It's a little _________________, to be honest.

Betty: Why's that? I love **Valentine's Day**! It's my _______________ favorite holiday.

Michael: Well, my mom always gets me a card with **roses** on it.

Betty: That's ___________. She sounds like fun. Well, do you want this card or not?

Michael: Yeah, I _______________ so. It's __________ than **roses** again! Thanks, Betty.

**B. Look at the bolded words in the dialog above. With a partner, think of some new information to replace these words.**

**C. Practice the dialog using the new information.**

## 2 Picture Description

**Listen and choose the statement that best describes what you see in the picture.** Track 21

1. 

Ⓐ Ⓑ Ⓒ Ⓓ

2. 

Ⓐ Ⓑ Ⓒ Ⓓ

## 3 Unscramble

**Unscramble the sentences below.**

1. like two / I'd / please. / baguettes,
   → ______________________________

2. Harry / champion. / is a / kickboxing / five-time
   → ______________________________

3. the year. / October is / the tenth / of / month
   → ______________________________

4. Today is / twenty-year / anniversary. / wedding / their
   → ______________________________

5. the / this year. / This is / fifth time / the / movie theater / I've been to
   → ______________________________

# Note Taking

| Main Points | Detail |
| --- | --- |
| | |
| | |
| | |
| | |
| | |
| | |

| Summary |
| --- |
| |
| |
| |
| |
| |
| |

# Brainstorming

# Journal/Activity Writing

# UNIT 06 The Weather

Warm-Up

What is the hottest place you have ever been?
Do you like playing in the snow?

**Talking About:**
Types of weather and the seasons

## 1 Model Dialog

**Listen and practice the dialog with a partner.** Track 22

**Angela:** Oh, are you back from England already? How was it?
**Freddy:** Yes, I got back yesterday. It was great.
**Angela:** I'm glad. What about the weather? I heard their weather is really bad.
**Freddy:** The weather was good, actually. I don't like it when it's too hot.
**Angela:** I love hot weather. The hotter the better! So, did it rain?
**Freddy:** On my last day, yeah. It rained cats and dogs!
**Angela:** Oh, that's too bad. Did you get wet?
**Freddy:** I got soaked to the bone. But it was fun.
**Angela:** Well, that's good! Are you glad to be back again?
**Freddy:** I guess so. But I'm a little under the weather. I think I have a cold.

### Speaking Success!

English has many **idioms** about and related to the weather.

**It rained cats and dogs.**
= *It rained heavily.*
**Soaked to the bone**
= *To be very wet*
**Under the weather**
= *Not feeling well*
**Take a rain check**
= *To postpone something*

## 2 Vocabulary

**A.** **Write the correct weather-related word or phrase beneath each picture.**

| rainy | clear/sunny | partly cloudy | hot and humid | cloudy |
|---|---|---|---|---|
| snowy | windy | cool | warm | freezing |

1. ______________

2. ______________

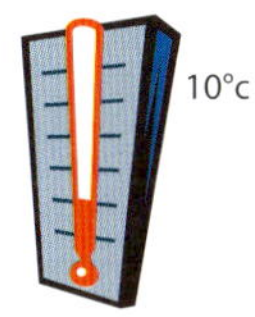


3. ______________

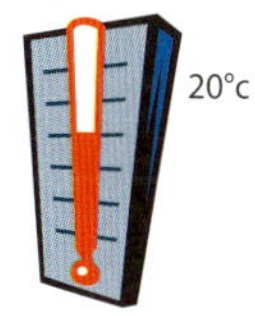


4. ______________

5. ______________

6. ______________

7. ______________

8. ______________

9. ______________

10. ______________

**B.** **Work with a partner. Make sentences about the weather. Use the words above.**

*When it is **rainy**, I like to stay inside and watch old movies.*

## 3 Essential Expressions

**Look at the sentences below. Fill in the blanks with the following words.**

| winds | hot and humid | snowy |
|---|---|---|
| rainy | freezing | clear |

1. The weather will be ______________ today, so bring an umbrella.
2. When the weather is ______________ outside, I love to stay at home in the air conditioning.
3. On a ______________ day, you can see France from my house!
4. It's ______________ out there, so make sure to wrap up and stay warm.
5. I love to go sledding on the hill by my house when it's ______________ outside.
6. Be careful out there. I heard on the news that there are strong ______________.

# 4 Listening

**A.** **Listen to John talk about his previous vacations. Write his responses.** Track 23

**Place A**

1. Where? ______________________
2. How long? ______________________
3. Weather? ______________________
4. Good time? ______________________

**Place B**

1. Where? ______________________
2. How long? ______________________
3. Weather? ______________________
4. Good time? ______________________

**Place C**

1. Where? ______________________
2. How long? ______________________
3. Weather? ______________________
4. Good time? ______________________

**B.** **Work in a group. Would you like to go to any of the places John visited? Which place has your favorite type of weather?**

*I hate hot weather, so I wouldn't want to go to Shanghai. I'd go to . . .*

**C.** **Work with a partner. Ask and answer the following questions. Write the answers below.**

1. Where did you go? ______________________
2. How long did you stay there? ______________________
3. What was the weather like? ______________________
4. Did you have a good time? ______________________

## 5 Questionnaire

**A. Ask three classmates the following questions and discover their personalities.**

1. **It is a hot and humid day. How do you cool yourself down?**
   a. I buy an ice cream for myself and my friends.
   b. I stay at home with the air conditioning on.
   c. I go to the swimming pool.

2. **There is a snow day! Class is canceled because of heavy snow. What do you do?**
   a. Stay at home and do your homework.
   b. Stay inside and watch television.
   c. Play in the snow with your friends.

3. **The weather forecaster says that a heavy storm is coming. What do you do?**
   a. Check that you have enough food.
   b. Order a pizza.
   c. Go to the park to play soccer.

4. **There is heavy rain. The news says it is not safe to drive, but you have an important appointment. What do you do?**
   a. Make a phone call to cancel your appointment.
   b. Forget the appointment and play video games.
   c. Drive to your appointment anyway.

5. **There is a flood! You are safe in your home, but you see a woman who is in danger. What do you do?**
   a. Call the police.
   b. Ignore her and make some coffee.
   c. Try to help her.

***If you answered:***

Mostly A: You are a kind and sensible person, if a little boring.

Mostly B: You are lazy and selfish, but at least you are safe.

Mostly C: You are a fun and interesting person, but also reckless and dangerous.

**B. Talk again to one of the classmates you spoke to above. What do you think about their choices? Would you make the same ones?**

*You said that you would drive to your appointment even if the roads were not safe. I think this is foolish and . . .*

**C. As a class, ask your teacher the above questions. What would he/she do in the above situations?**

## 6 Partner-Up

**A.** **Work with a partner. Partner A looks at this page and partner B looks at page 129. Take turns asking each other questions about the weather. Write the answers in the spaces.**

### WEATHER AROUND THE WORLD

#### Partner A

What's the weather like in SYDNEY in MARCH?

SYDNEY—MARCH
- 
- 
- 

HONOLULU—AUGUST
- It's hot and a bit humid.
- It doesn't rain much.
- The high is about 31 and the low is about 23.

BANGKOK—APRIL
- 
- 
- 

SAPPORO—FEBRUARY
- It's cold.
- It snows a lot.
- The high is about 0 and the low is about -9.

LONDON—JULY
- 
- 
- 

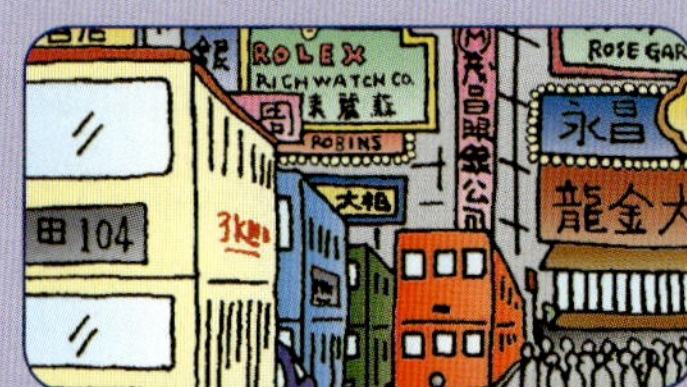


HONG KONG—MARCH
- It's cool.
- It rains sometimes.
- The high is about 20 and the low is about 10.

AUCKLAND—JUNE
- 
- 
- 

GUAM—JANUARY
- It's hot and humid.
- It doesn't rain much.
- The high is about 32 and the low is about 25.

SAN FRANCISCO—JULY
- 
- 
- 

**B.** **Have you visited any of these places? Would you like to? Discuss this with your partner.**

*I would love to visit San Francisco. On TV it always looks sunny, and . . .*

# Integrated Learning

## 1 Comprehension

A. Think about the weather in your country in each of the four seasons. Write keywords in the boxes below.

| SPRING | SUMMER |
|---|---|
| | |

| FALL / AUTUMN | WINTER |
|---|---|
| | |

B. Choose one of the four seasons. Write a short paragraph about this season in your country. Use the keywords above.

Spring in the Netherlands is my favorite time of the year. The skies are blue, and the weather is cool but not too hot or cold. I can hear birds singing and see new flowers in the ground. It is my favorite season.

C. Present your writing to the class. Answer any questions they might have.

D. Role-Play: Look outside. What is the weather like? Pretend you are a weather forecaster, and give the forecast to your partner.

*It looks like it will rain today. I would recommend that you stay . . .*

# Practice

## 1 Dialog

**A. Listen to the recording and put the missing words into the dialog.** Track 22

| glad | guess | already | weather |
|---|---|---|---|
| yeah | under | better | yesterday |

Angela: Oh, are you back from **England** _______________? How was it?

Takeshi: Yes, I got back _________________. It was great.

Angela: I'm ________. What about the weather? I heard their weather is really **bad**.

Takeshi: The weather was **good**, actually. I don't like it when it's too **hot**.

Angela: I love hot ______________. The hotter the ____________! So, did it rain?

Takeshi: On my last day, ________. It rained cats and dogs!

Angela: Oh, that's too bad. Did you get wet?

Takeshi: I got **soaked to the bone**. But it was fun.

Angela: Well, that's good! Are you glad to be back again?

Takeshi: I ___________ so. But I'm a little _________ the weather. I think I have a cold.

**B. Look at the bolded words in the dialog above. With a partner, think of some new information to replace these words.**

**C. Practice the dialog using the new information.**

## 2 Picture Description

**Listen and choose the statement that best describes what you see in the picture.** Track 24

1.

Ⓐ Ⓑ Ⓒ Ⓓ

2.

Ⓐ Ⓑ Ⓒ Ⓓ

## 3 Unscramble

**Unscramble the sentences below.**

1. today. / It is / very hot / a / day

→ ____________________

2. train arrives / 6:05 p.m. / The / at

→ ____________________

3. is cold / today. / It / out there

→ ____________________

4. a coat / Wear / go outside. / when you

→ ____________________

5. roads are / The / slippery. / very

→ ____________________

# Note Taking

| Main Points | Detail |
|---|---|
| | |
| | |
| | |
| | |
| | |
| | |

| Summary |
|---|
| |
| |
| |
| |
| |
| |

# Brainstorming

# Journal/Activity Writing

# UNIT 07 Food

Warm-Up

What did you have for breakfast today?
What is a food that you haven't eaten but would love to try?

**Talking About:**
Different types of food

## 1 Model Dialog

**Listen and practice the dialog with a partner.** Track 25

**Jean-Paul:** Melissa, do we have any milk left?

**Melissa:** I think so. There was some this morning when I had my breakfast.

**Jean-Paul:** Hmm. There's none in the fridge. Should I get some?

**Melissa:** Yes, please. Can you get some bananas as well?

**Jean-Paul:** Bananas? Sure, I'll make a shopping list before I go.

**Melissa:** OK, we need yogurt, bread, eggs . . . that's all I can think of.

**Jean-Paul:** Do we have any cola? I really have a craving.

**Melissa:** Cola? That's really bad for your teeth, you know.

**Jean-Paul:** Well, I'll buy some toothpaste, too! By the way, two friends of mine are coming for dinner tonight.

**Melissa:** OK. Then we should pick up some wine, too.

### Speaking Success!

We use the phrase *by the way* when we **change the topic** of a conversation.

Great! Let's go. **By the way**, two friends of mine are coming for dinner tonight.

I just started a new job. **By the way**, I moved to a new apartment.

## 2 Vocabulary

**A. Match these food names to the correct pictures.**

| chocolate | milk | carrot | corn | avocado | lemon | onion | butter |
|---|---|---|---|---|---|---|---|
| coffee | bread | apple | celery | broccoli | egg | banana | mushroom |

**B. Which of these foods do you like? Which don't you like? Discuss with a partner.**

*I like **chocolate**, and I hate **lemons** . . .*

## 3 Essential Expressions

**Look at the sentences below. Fill in the blanks with the following words.**

| take | onions | celery | fruits |
|---|---|---|---|
| bread | market | toppings | |

1. I made a pizza with corn and bacon for ________________.
2. Lisa made me pasta with ________________ and mushrooms.
3. I want a slice of ________________ and butter and some chocolate milk for breakfast.
4. The only vegetable I really hate is ________________—yuck!
5. She made a really nice salad with some avocado we got from the ________________.
6. Do you ________________ milk with your coffee?
7. The only ________________ that looked nice were the bananas and apples, so we got those.

## 4 Listening

**A. Listen to Tony talking about his favorite foods. Write his responses below.** Track 26

1. Name Tony's five favorite foods.
______________________________
2. Which healthy foods does Tony like?
______________________________
3. Which food does Tony hate?
______________________________
4. Why does he not like it?
______________________________
5. Why doesn't Tony like chocolate?
______________________________
6. Which food can Tony cook himself?
______________________________
7. What is Tony's perfect meal?
______________________________

**B. Listen again. Write a number next to each food in the order it is mentioned.**

| | |
|---|---|
| 1. hamburgers _____ | 2. pizza _____ |
| 3. ice cream _____ | 4. egg _____ |
| 5. cabbage _____ | 6. gravy _____ |
| 7. roast beef _____ | 8. broccoli _____ |

**C. Tony's perfect meal is roast beef with Yorkshire puddings. What would be your perfect meal? Discuss with a partner.**

*My perfect meal? Let me see . . . mashed potatoes, fried chicken . . .*

## 5 Survey

**A.** **Walk around your classroom. Find three classmates for each of the statements below. Write their names in the chart.**

**Find a classmate who . . .**

| | Name | Name | Name |
|---|---|---|---|
| . . . doesn't like chocolate. | | | |
| . . . can make pizza. | | | |
| . . . loves chicken. | | | |
| . . . can't boil an egg. | | | |
| . . . has never tried Indian food. | | | |
| . . . hates spicy food. | | | |
| . . . has eaten until he/she was sick. | | | |
| . . . is on a diet. | | | |
| . . . eats fast food every week. | | | |
| . . . drinks coffee. | | | |
| . . . loves Italian food. | | | |
| . . . has eaten more than four plates of food at a buffet. | | | |
| . . . doesn't eat breakfast. | | | |
| . . . has eaten a whole pizza. | | | |
| . . . is a vegetarian. | | | |

**B.** **Choose one of the classmates you spoke to above. Ask these questions and think of your own.**

1. What is the most disgusting thing you have ever eaten?
2. What is a food that you would eat for every meal if you could?
3. What is the most unhealthy food you can think of?

## 6 Partner-Up

**A.** **Mike and Dave eat a lot! Partner A looks at this page and partner B looks at page 130. Ask your partner the questions and then add up the score. Who won?**

| How many . . . | Amount | How many . . . | Amount |
|---|---|---|---|
| 1. . . . bananas did he eat? | | 2. . . . apples did he eat? | |
| 3. . . . eggs did he eat? | | 4. . . . bowls of rice did he eat? | |
| 5. . . . boxes of cookies did he eat? | | 6. . . . slices of pizza did he eat? | |
| 7. . . . pieces of cake did he eat? | | 8. . . . bags of potato chips did he eat? | |
| 9. . . . glasses of milk did he drink? | | 10. . . . bottles of cola did he drink? | |
| 11. . . . cups of coffee did he drink? | | 12. . . . cans of juice did he drink? | |
| | | Dave's score = | |

**B.** **Look again at the food that Mike and Dave have eaten. Which of the food types are countable and which are uncountable?**

*Dave drank three bottles of cola and two apples. Cola is uncountable and . . .*

**C.** **Now look at how much food each person has left. Who has more food left over?**

*Dave has two boxes of chocolate chip cookies left. He also has two bananas and . . .*

# Integrated Learning

## 1 Comprehension

**A. Fill in the blanks in the dialog with the words below.**

some any thirsty slice hungry glass

Colin: Hey, I am pretty ________. Is there ________ food?

Sally: I think there is ________ pizza in the refrigerator.

Colin: Great! I'll have a ________ of pizza.

Sally: If you're ________, there is a ________ of water, too.

Colin: Thanks!

### Grammar Note

- Use *some* when it's not important to say the number of something.

  *Some bananas. Some milk.*

- Use *any* for questions and negatives.

  *Is there any cheese?*

**B. Work with a partner. Partner A looks below and partner B looks at page 131. Give hints to help your partner guess each word, but do not say the word.**

It's a fruit. It's oval and yellow. It tastes sour— *A lemon!*

| What is it? | What shape is it? | How big is it? | What color is it? | How does it taste? | What is it like? |
|---|---|---|---|---|---|
| It's a kind of fruit. / vegetable. / drink. / snack. / food. | It's round. / oval. / square. / long. | It's big. / pretty big. / pretty small. / small. | It's green / yellow / brown / pink / red — inside. / outside. | It's sweet. / sour. / salty. / bitter. | It's light. / heavy. / soft. / hard. / juicy. |

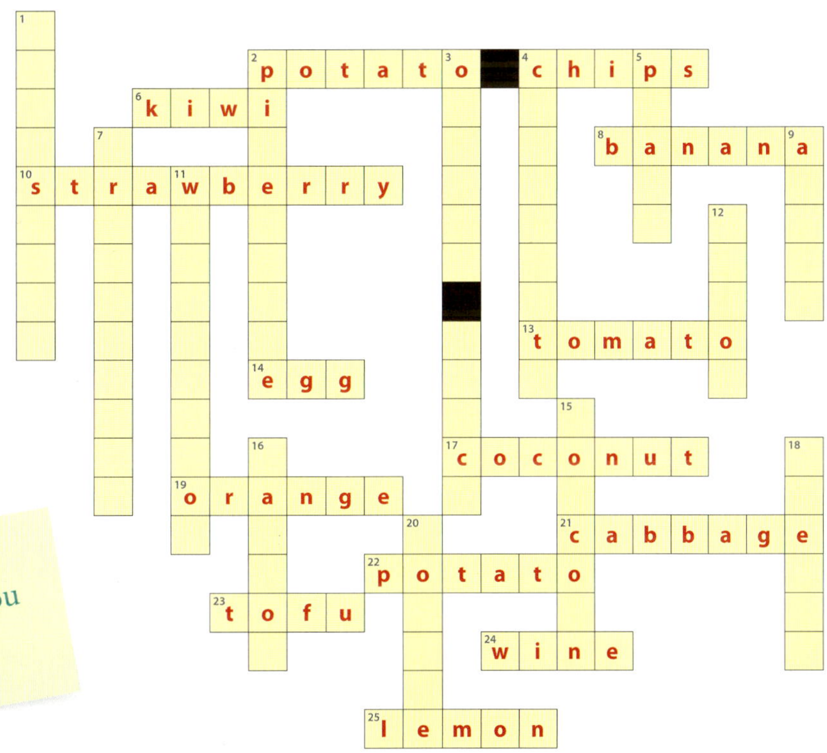


How do you spell it?

Partner A

# Practice

## 1 Dialog

**A. Listen to the recording and put the missing words into the dialog.** Track 25

| yogurt | toothpaste | morning | none |
|---|---|---|---|
| craving | pick | before | coming |

**Jean-Paul:** Melissa, do we have any **milk** left?

**Melissa:** I think so. There was some this ______________ when I had my breakfast.

**Jean-Paul:** Hmm. There's _________ in the fridge. Should I get some?

**Melissa:** Yes, please. Can you get some **bananas** as well?

**Jean-Paul:** **Bananas**? Sure, I'll make a shopping list ____________ I go.

**Melissa:** OK, we need _________, bread, eggs . . . that's all I can think of.

**Jean-Paul:** Do we have any **cola**? I really have a ___________.

**Melissa:** **Cola**? That's really bad for your teeth, you know.

**Jean-Paul:** Well, I'll buy some ________________, too! By the way, two friends of mine are ____________ for dinner tonight.

**Melissa:** OK. Then we should ________ up some **wine**, too.

**B. Look at the bolded words in the dialog above. With a partner, think of some new information to replace these words.**

**C. Practice the dialog using the new information.**

## 2 Picture Description

**Listen and choose the statement that best describes what you see in the picture.** Track 27

1.

Ⓐ Ⓑ Ⓒ Ⓓ

2.

Ⓐ Ⓑ Ⓒ Ⓓ

## 3 Unscramble

**Unscramble the sentences below.**

1. three / I bought / melons / the store. / from

→ ______________________________

2. two large / Between us, / pizzas. / we ate

→ ______________________________

3. please. / of / I'll have / brown bread, / one loaf

→ ______________________________

4. gave five / charity drive. / to the / We / cans of beans

→ ______________________________

5. of dinner. / had two / I / helpings

→ ______________________________

## Note Taking

| Main Points | Detail |
| --- | --- |
| | |
| | |
| | |
| | |
| | |
| | |

| Summary |
| --- |
| |
| |
| |
| |
| |
| |

## Brainstorming

# Journal/Activity Writing

# UNIT 08 Describing People

Talking About:
What people look like and how they act

**Warm-Up**

How would you describe your own personality in three words?
What would your perfect partner look like?

## 1 Model Dialog

**Listen and practice the dialog with a partner.** Track 28

**Rafael:** Katie, do you still want to go on that blind date with my friend?

**Katie:** Yeah, I do. I'm a bit nervous, though. What does he look like?

**Rafael:** Well, he's taller than me. And he has shoulder-length hair.

**Katie:** Oh, that sounds nice. What about his eyes?

**Rafael:** His eye color? I don't know. I've never really looked. Maybe blue.

**Katie:** Blue? Wow, that's great. And is he a nice guy?

**Rafael:** He's a great guy. I've known him for a long time.

**Katie:** Well, I hope he's friendly and funny. I like guys who are funny.

**Rafael:** He always makes me laugh. But I laugh at everything!

**Katie:** And one more thing—I hope he's punctual! I hate waiting.

### Speaking Success!

It is considered informal to start a sentence with a **conjunction**. However, it is not incorrect, and is common in spoken language.

**And** one more thing . . .
**But** you told me I had to!
**Or** we could go there tomorrow.

## 2 Vocabulary

**A. Look at these words for describing people. Practice saying them out loud.**

**B. Work with a partner. Use these words to describe your classmates.**

*Jeff is **average height** and quite **skinny**. He has **long sideburns** and . . .*

## 3 Essential Expressions

**Look at the sentences below. Fill in the blanks with the following words.**

| bald | tall | overweight | wear glasses |
|---|---|---|---|
| cute | freckles | dark complexion | muscular |

1. I've been going to the gym a lot recently, so I've started to get really ________________.
2. I used to be ________________ and that's why I decided to exercise and eat healthier.
3. My best friend is really ________________ so I feel short compared to her.
4. When my dad was young, he had a lot of hair, but now he is ________________!
5. My sister has a lot of light brown ________________ all over her face.
6. You have such a ________________ baby! She looks like a doll!
7. I used to have good eyesight, but now I need to ________________.
8. Thanks to her ________________, she doesn't get sunburns easily.

## 4 Listening

**A. Listen to Ben describe some people who are important to him. Complete the sentences with his descriptions of their appearance.** Track 29

**1. Mother**

a. She has __________ __________ hair.

b. She has a __________ face.

**2. Father**

a. He weighs __________ pounds.

b. He has a really __________ __________.

**3. Best Friend**

a. He is __________ feet tall.

b. He has __________ __________ eyes.

**4. Ideal Partner**

a. She is __________ foot __________.

b. She has__________ __________ eyes.

**5. Favorite Actor**

a. His name is __________ __________.

b. He has a __________ right above his __________.

**B. Listen again. Match the people to Ben's descriptions of their personalities.**

| | |
|---|---|
| 1. He is really funny, and really lazy sometimes. • | • a. father |
| 2. I think he is very kind and outgoing. • | • b. best friend |
| 3. She is honest and kind. • | • c. favorite actor |
| 4. She is very hard-working and polite. • | • d. ideal partner |
| 5. He can be rude, but he is never boring! • | • e. mother |

**C. Work with a partner. Describe your own parents, best friend, favorite actor, and ideal partner.**

*My father is tall and he is going bald! He can be quite strict, but he is also . . .*

## 5 Survey

**A.** **Fill in the chart below with words to describe people.**

| | |
|---|---|
| Height | |
| Body type | |
| Age | |
| Hair | |
| Face | |
| Complexion | |
| Eyes | |
| Personality | |

**B.** **Find three classmates you do not usually speak to. Looking at their appearance, fill in this chart with the words to describe them.**

| | Name ________ | Name ________ | Name ________ |
|---|---|---|---|
| Height | | | |
| Body Type | | | |
| Age | | | |
| Hair | | | |
| Face | | | |
| Complexion | | | |
| Eyes | | | |
| Personality | | | |

**C.** **Work in a group. Describe one of your classmates. Your team members will try to guess who that person is.**

*This person is tall and skinny, with medium-length black hair and a pale complexion . . .*

## 6 Partner-Up

**A. Listen to the dialog and perform both roles with a partner.** Track 30

**Male Student:** Hey, **Stacy**, how was class today?
**Female Student:** Oh, **terrible**. I had **Mr. Wallace**. He's so **mean**.
**Male Student:** **Mr. Wallace**? I know the name, what does he look like?
**Female Student:** He's quite **short**, and he has **a thick mustache**.
**Male Student:** I know him. He always wears **a yellow sweater**.
**Female Student:** That's him! He always **gives us so much homework**.
**Male Student:** That's **too bad**. I just had **Mrs. Chigwell**.
**Female Student:** Oh. She's **great**, isn't she?
**Male Student:** Yeah, definitely.

**B. With your partner, practice the dialog with the following details.**

- Scarlett
- brilliant
- Mr. Epsom
- funny
- chubby
- blond hair
- a pink bow tie
- makes me laugh
- great
- Miss Balham
- boring

- Joan
- really bad
- Mr. French
- annoying
- tall
- thick glasses
- brown boots
- shouts at me
- a shame
- Ms. Black
- great

- Dora
- tiring
- Mr. Johnson
- tiring
- skinny
- a bald head
- a tweed jacket
- makes us stay late
- unlucky
- Miss Waters
- so much fun

**C. Talk about your own favorite and least favorite teachers. Practice the dialog again, using your own experiences.**

# Integrated Learning

## 1 Comprehension

**A.** Look at the pictures and descriptions below. Write the correct letter beneath each picture.

**A** She's around 20. She's tall, slim, and beautiful. She has long, straight black hair.

**B** He's in his 40s. He's short and overweight. He has a moustache and a beard.

**C** She's really cute. She has medium-length wavy hair and big, beautiful eyes.

**D** He's average height and average build. He has a ponytail.

**E** She's around 60. She has short curly hair and wears glasses.

**F** He has a wide face and a dark complexion. He's very muscular.

**B.** Look at this casting call for a Hollywood movie. Think of a movie and its main character. Write your own casting call.

**Actors Wanted!**
We are looking for actors for a new action movie, *Kiss of Life*. We require a tall, muscular male actor in his forties to play the lead role, Butch MacFarlane. We would prefer blond hair, but any color will do. The character will be rude, funny, and aggressive! If this sounds like you, then please contact us now at *manfighter@holly.wood*.

**C.** Work in a group. Describe your favorite celebrity or fictional character. Your teammates must try to guess who you are talking about.

He is a small boy, and he wears round glasses. He has brown hair and a scar— *Harry Potter!*

# Practice

## 1 Dialog

**A.** Listen to the recording and put the missing words into the dialog. Track 28

| nervous | funny | great | blind |
|---|---|---|---|
| laugh | still | color | punctual |

**Rafael:** Katie, do you ________ want to go on that ________ date with my friend?

**Katie:** Yeah, I do. I'm a bit __________, though. What does he look like?

**Rafael:** Well, he's **taller** than me. And he has **shoulder-length** hair.

**Katie:** Oh, that sounds nice. What about his eyes?

**Rafael:** His eye ________? I don't know. I've never really looked. Maybe **blue**.

**Katie:** **Blue**? Wow, that's great. And is he a nice guy?

**Rafael:** He's a ____________ guy. I've known him for a long time.

**Katie:** Well, I hope he's **friendly** and ___________. I like guys who are funny.

**Rafael:** He always makes me __________. But I laugh at everything!

**Katie:** And one more thing—I hope he's ___________! I hate waiting.

**B.** Look at the bolded words in the dialog above. With a partner, think of some new information to replace these words.

**C.** Practice the dialog using the new information.

## 2 Picture Description

**Listen and choose the statement that best describes what you see in the picture.** Track 31

1.

Ⓐ Ⓑ Ⓒ Ⓓ

2.

Ⓐ Ⓑ Ⓒ Ⓓ

## 3 Unscramble

**Unscramble the sentences below.**

1. dishonest / He is / and rude.
   → ______________________________

2. a little / I might / disorganized, / be / not lazy. / but I'm
   → ______________________________

3. new student / seems very / The / shy.
   → ______________________________

4. outgoing. / She is / talkative / very / and
   → ______________________________

5. sister can / shy, / be / but sometimes / My / outgoing / as well.
   → ______________________________

## Note Taking

| Main Points | Detail |
| --- | --- |
| | |
| | |
| | |
| | |
| | |
| | |

| Summary |
| --- |
| |
| |
| |
| |
| |
| |

## Brainstorming

# Journal/Activity Writing

# UNIT 09 Shopping

Warm-Up

Do you like shopping?
How often do you go shopping?

**Talking About:**
Going shopping

## 1 Model Dialog

**Listen and practice the dialog with a partner.** Track 32

**Sue:** Wow, I love your sunglasses! Where did you get them?

**Nathan:** Thanks. I got them from a fashion outlet store.

**Sue:** Oh, an outlet store, that's good! Where is it? Were they cheap?

**Nathan:** It's not far from here actually, on 6th Street. They were $50.

**Sue:** $50? Wow, that's good. My last pair of sunglasses cost a lot more!

**Nathan:** Yeah, the fashion outlet has lots of great stuff, and the prices are good, too.

**Sue:** Oh, I'll have to go there soon. I need a new pair of jeans.

**Nathan:** Would you like to go there now? I'm not busy.

**Sue:** Oh, great! Do you want to have coffee first? I need a rest.

**Nathan:** No problem. Could you pay for me? I left my wallet at home!

### Speaking Success!

If you are asked **two questions** at the same time, simply respond to them in the order they were asked.

**Where is it?**
**Were they cheap?**
It's on 6th street.
They were $50.

**How are you?**
**When did you get here?**
I'm good, thanks. I got here five minutes ago.

## 2 Vocabulary

**A. Match the stores with the descriptions.**

| | |
|---|---|
| 1. electronics store • | • a. This store sells a wide range of food and household goods. |
| 2. grocery • | • b. A place that sells used items. |
| 3. pharmacy • | • c. You could buy a television here. |
| 4. furniture store • | • d. This store sells only fresh fruits and vegetables. |
| 5. shoe store • | • e. A place that sells medicine. |
| 6. second-hand store • | • f. This store specializes in footwear. |
| 7. supermarket • | • g. You could buy a table and chairs here. |

**B. Work with a partner. Which of these stores would you like to go to?**

*I would like to go to the* ***second-hand store****. They have good deals.*

## 3 Essential Expressions

**Look at the sentences below. Fill in the blanks with the following words.**

| shoe store | pharmacy | supermarket | grocery |
|---|---|---|---|
| electronics store | furniture store | second-hand store | |

1. I get all of my fresh fruit and vegetables from the ________________ store.
2. I saw a great pair of sneakers ________________, but they didn't have them in my size.
3. I do all of my shopping at the ________________, as they sell everything I need.
4. We spent the day looking for a new sofa in the ________________.
5. I went to the ________________ to pick up my prescription.
6. We want a new TV, so we will go to the ________________ to look for one tomorrow.
7. You can get lots of bargains on old clothes at the ________________.

# 4 Listening

**A. Listen and write the numbers that you hear. Compare your answers with a partner.**

Track 33

1. ______________
2. ______________
3. ______________
4. ______________
5. ______________
6. ______________
7. ______________
8. ______________

**B. Listen to a radio interview with the owner of a new store. Complete the sentences below.**

Track 34

1. The owner of the store is ______________.
2. The name of the store is ________, ________, ________.
3. The store opens this ________, October ________.
4. At first they will sell only ________, but they might sell some unique ________ later on.
5. Shoes will cost from $________ to $________.
6. As well as women's shoes, they will have ________ and ______________, too.
7. For their ________ week, all shoes will be ________% cheaper.

**C. Work in a group. What is your favorite store? Give your opinions on each other's choices.**

*My favorite store is a music store in my town. It has been open for seventy years, and . . .*

## 5 Class Game

**A.** **Let's play a game! Play a game with your class based on the American TV show *The Price Is Right.***

- Your teacher will think of a price for the following items.
- Look at each item and guess how much it is worth.
- Your teacher will say the correct price.
- The student who guesses the closest to the correct price—without going over—is the winner!

### Game 1

My guess: $ ______

AXUS Widescreen TV

- forty-inch screen
- TFT active matrix display
- clear picture at any angle

### Game 2

My guess: $ ______

Cordless Telephone Z15

- 100-number memory
- alarm function
- hands-free speaking ability

### Game 3

My guess: $ ______

Washer Apricot C4A

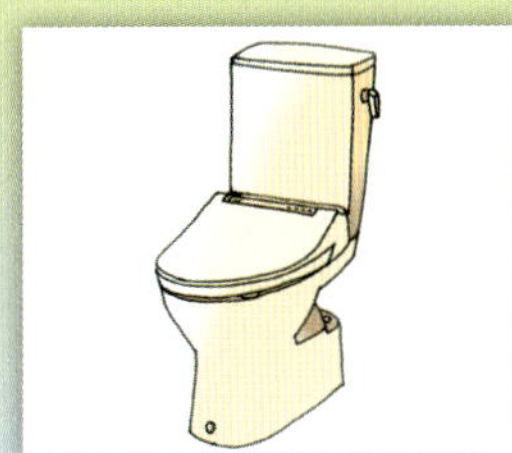

- includes bidet
- wireless remote control
- self-cleaning

### Game 4

My guess: $ ______

FutureNet Notebook

- stylish design
- fast processing power
- advanced graphics

### Game 5

My guess: $ ______

Powerfax UF 330

- multifunction fax machine
- inkjet
- 100-page paper tray

### Game 6

My guess: $ ______

Mini Cam PC121

- wireless Internet access
- glass lens
- nearly eight-hour battery life

### Game 7

My guess: $ ______

Super Deluxe Rice Cooker

- top-of-the-line model
- five-layer stainless steel body
- liquid crystal display

### Game 8

My guess: $ ______

160GB MP3 player

- large storage
- high sound quality
- top-quality earphones

**B.** **Now play in a group. Think of your own four items. Give them a name and mention three functions for each. Your teammates will try to guess.**

*This is a flat-screen computer monitor. It is full HD! It also has 3D and a thirty-inch screen . . .*

## 6 Partner-Up

**A. Work with a partner. Look at the dialogs below. Circle the lines that best fit each dialog. Then, practice the dialogs together.**

### Buying a Shirt

**Customer:** Excuse me. I'm looking for a shirt.

**Clerk:**
i. What kind of shirt are you interested in?
ii. What size shoes?

**Customer:**
a. Short-sleeved.
b. Do you have any jeans?

**Clerk:** We have many different short-sleeved shirts.

**Customer:**
a. Hmm . . . can I try one on?
b. About $30 to $40.

**Clerk:**
i. Sure. The dressing room's over there.
ii. No, it's not on sale.

### Bargaining for Shoes

**Clerk:** Hello. May I help you?

**Customer:**
a. See you later.
b. Umm . . . yes. Do you have these in black?

**Clerk:**
i. You like black? I hate it!
ii. I'm sorry. we're out of that color. We have gray and blue.

**Customer:**
a. How much are these gray ones?
b. I hate red.

**Clerk:**
i. $90.
ii. They're free. Take them.

**Customer:**
a. Can you give me a discount?
b. Are you crazy?

**Clerk:**
i. Yes, we do. But I won't show them to you.
ii. OK. I'll give them to you for $80.

**Customer:**
a. Give them to me for free.
b. Hmm . . . that's too expensive. How about $50?

**Clerk:**
i. OK, then, $50.
ii. We don't accept credit cards.

**Customer:**
a. It doesn't fit.
b. Good. I'll take them.

**B. Role-Play: Use these two dialogs as an example. With your partner, think of a different shopping situation.**

**C. Perform your role-play for the class.**

*Hello, ma'am. How may I help you today? . . .*

# Integrated Learning

## 1 Comprehension

**A.** **Work with a partner. The cards on pages 132-133 have many useful shopping expressions. Read out each sentence and think of a response.**

**Sample Responses:**

- It's five thousand won.
- That item is $30.
- I'm not sure, let me find out.
- It's on sale today, for only $12.

**B.** **Now, your teacher will read out each card. Each pair will give their answer. The teacher will choose the team with the best answer. That team wins the number of points on the card.**

**C.** **Look again at the cards. With your partner, prepare an original role-play using at least two expressions from each set of cards.**

Write notes for your role-play below.

**D.** **Perform your role-play for the class.**

Excuse me. Can you help me, please? *Yes, of course.* Oh good, I'd like to return this . . .

# Practice

## 1 Dialog

**A. Listen to the recording and put the missing words into the dialog.** Track 32

| coffee | good | problem | outlet |
|---|---|---|---|
| fashion | prices | Thanks | wallet |

Sue: Wow, I love your **sunglasses**! Where did you get them?

Nathan: ___________. I got them from a fashion ___________ store.

Sue: Oh, an outlet store, that's ________! Where is it? Were they cheap?

Nathan: It's not far from here actually, on **6$^{th}$ Street**. They were **$50**.

Sue: **$50**? Wow, that's good. My last **pair of sunglasses** cost a lot more!

Nathan: Yeah, the ___________ outlet has lots of great stuff, and the ________ are good, too.

Sue: Oh, I'll have to go there soon. I need a new **pair of jeans**.

Nathan: Would you like to go there now? I'm not busy.

Sue: Oh, great! Do you want to have ________ first? I need a rest.

Nathan: No ___________. Can you pay for me? I left my ___________ at home!

**B. Look at the bolded words in the dialog above. With a partner, think of some new information to replace these words.**

**C. Practice the dialog using the new information.**

## 2 Picture Description

**Listen and choose the statement that best describes what you see in the picture.** Track 35

1. 

Ⓐ Ⓑ Ⓒ Ⓓ

2. 

Ⓐ Ⓑ Ⓒ Ⓓ

## 3 Unscramble

**Unscramble the sentences below.**

1. ma'am? / help you, / May I
   → ______________________

2. you / How can / today? / I help
   → ______________________

3. ask you / May I / time the / starts? / what / show
   → ______________________

4. my homework. / can help you / finish / I / after I
   → ______________________

5. may I / How / today, / help you / sir?
   → ______________________

# Note Taking

| Main Points | Detail |
| --- | --- |
| | |
| | |
| | |
| | |
| | |
| | |

| Summary |
| --- |
| |
| |
| |
| |
| |
| |

# Brainstorming

# Journal/Activity Writing

# UNIT 10 Movies & Television

Warm-Up

How many hours of television do you watch a week?
When was the last time you went to the movie theater?

**Talking About:**
Our favorite movies, TV programs, and actors

## 1 Model Dialog

**Listen and practice the dialog with a partner.** Track 36

**Steven:** Are you busy this weekend, Marie?

**Marie:** Actually, I do have plans on Saturday. I'm going to the movies.

**Steven:** Oh, really? What are you going to see? Anything fun?

**Marie:** I'm gonna see *Je t'aime, Mon Amour*. It's a romance film.

**Steven:** Oh, I heard about that. The French one, right? I heard good things.

**Marie:** Would you like to join me? I haven't booked the tickets yet.

**Steven:** Well, I'm not really a fan of romance movies. I prefer action and comedy.

**Marie:** That's a shame. I like all kinds of movies, actually, not just romance.

**Steven:** When the next *Captain Adventure* movie comes out, would you like to see it?

**Marie:** Guy Francis is in that, right? He's so handsome.

**Speaking Success!**

*Do* can be used in a sentence for **emphasis**.

I **do** have plans on Saturday.
She **does** look lovely today.
I **do** want to come with you.

## 2 Vocabulary

**A. Match the movie genres with their descriptions.**

horror comedy action animation science-fiction romance fantasy documentary

**This movie genre . . .**

1. . . . is usually set in the future, and features amazing technology. ____________
2. . . . features explosions, car chases, and exciting scenes. ____________
3. . . . tries to make us laugh as much as possible. ____________
4. . . . is very scary and often violent. ____________
5. . . . has magic and fantastic creatures. ____________
6. . . . features a man and a woman who fall in love. ____________
7. . . . is usually aimed at children and features drawn characters. ____________
8. . . . tells us stories about real life. ____________

**B. Can you think of a movie that fits each of these genres? Discuss with a partner.**

*I can think of an* ***animated*** *movie—*Beauty and the Beast *by Disney. It's my favorite!*

## 3 Essential Expressions

**Look at the sentences below. Fill in the blanks with the following words.**

| fantasy | horror | romance | movies |
|---|---|---|---|
| animation | comedy | TV | action |

1. I like watching ____________ movies because I love to laugh.
2. Andy loves to scare himself by watching ____________ movies.
3. Lord of the Rings is my favorite ____________ movie series.
4. My girlfriend and I enjoy watching ____________ together at the theater.
5. Jake likes to watch the documentary channel on ____________.
6. ____________ movies are usually clichéd, but I love them because they are so exciting!
7. My brother loves watching all kinds of science-fiction ____________ from Japan.
8. I think ____________ movies are stupid, but my boyfriend loves them.

## 4 Listening

**A. Unscramble the sentences to make questions.**

1. do you like? / of movies / what kinds
______________________________
2. actress? / who is / actor or / your favorite
______________________________
3. you've ever / what's the best / seen? / movie
______________________________
4. the last movie / what was / you saw?
______________________________
5. how often / to the movies? / do you go
______________________________
6. more than once? / the same movie / have you ever seen
______________________________

**B. Listen to Darcy answer the questions from above. Write his answers below. Compare your answers with a partner.** Track 37

1. Darcy likes to watch ______________________________
2. Darcy's favorite actress is ______________________________
3. The best movie Darcy has ever seen is ______________________________
4. Which movie has Darcy watched more than once? ______________________________
5. Darcy thinks movies nowadays are so ______________________________
6. What was the last movie Darcy saw? ______________________________
7. Darcy thinks that people make movies way too ______________________________

**C. Work with a partner. Ask each other the unscrambled questions from Activity A.**

What kind of movies do you like?
*Oh, all kinds. But especially sci-fi and thrillers.*

## 5 Interview

**A. Work with a partner. Ask him/her the following questions. Write down the answers.**

### Movies

1. Have you seen any movie more than five times? What was it?
2. What is the worst movie you have ever seen?
3. How many times did you go to the movie theater last month?
4. What is your favorite animated movie?
5. Which upcoming movie are you excited to see?
6. What is the scariest movie you have ever seen?

### Television

1. On average, how many hours of TV do you watch a day?
2. What kinds of programs do you usually watch?
3. What's one of your favorite shows?
4. Do you ever watch any shows to help with your English?
5. What shows did you watch yesterday?
6. Do you prefer watching television or watching movies?

**B. Work in a group. Discuss your partner's responses with the group.**

*Ginny has seen* Star Wars *over ten times! She says the worst movie she has ever seen is . . .*

## 6 Partner-Up

**A. Listen to the dialog and perform both roles with a partner.** Track 38

**Husband:** I'm bored. What's on TV tonight? Is there anything good on?
**Wife:** Let's see . . . how about ***Real Life Weddings***?
**Husband:** I'm not crazy about **reality TV**. What else is on?
**Wife:** Well, we can watch the new season of ***Police Force***.
**Husband:** ***Police Force***? That sounds good. What kind of show is that?
**Wife:** It's **a drama**. I've heard that it's very good.
**Husband:** Great, let's watch that. What time is it on?
**Wife:** At **7:30 p.m.**, after the news.
**Husband:** Perfect! What channel is it on?
**Wife:** **Channel 6**. That's my favorite channel, actually.

**B. With your partner, practice the dialog with the following details.**

- *Life Cycles of Alaskan Salmon*
- documentaries
- *Man Hunter*
- an action show
- 9:50 p.m.
- BLAST

- *Little and Lord*
- sitcoms
- *Prince Regent*
- a costume drama
- 9:00 p.m.
- BTC

- *20 Questions*
- quiz shows
- *I Know You Love Me*
- a romantic comedy
- 6:20 p.m.
- L Channel

**C. Find out which television programs are showing tonight. Practice the above dialog with real-life examples.**

# Integrated Learning

## 1 Comprehension

**A. Listen to Kalani talking about movies. Fill in the answers below.** Track 39

1. Who is Kalani's favorite actress?

   ______________________________

2. Which male actor does she like?

   ______________________________

3. How often does Kalani go to the movies?

   ______________________________

4. Where does she borrow movies from?

   ______________________________

5. Which movie does she want to see again?

   ______________________________

**B. Look at the classic movie titles below. Read the descriptions of these classic movies and guess which movie is being described.**

*Titanic* *Jurassic Park* *Superman* *Jaws* *Harry Potter* *E.T.*

1. It's a movie about dinosaurs that have been brought to life. ____________
2. It's a movie about a small town which is facing danger from a killer shark. ____________
3. It's about a boy who goes to a special school to become a wizard. ____________
4. It's a movie about an alien that is lost on Earth and needs to get home. ____________
5. It's about a man who can fly and who saves people. ____________
6. It's a tragic love story which takes place on a giant cruise ship. ____________

**C. Work with a partner. Look at the dialog pattern below. Replace the underlined words to talk about a movie you have seen before.**

A: Have you seen *The Sixth Sense*?
B: Yes, I have. / No, I haven't. What's it about?
A: It's about a boy who can see dead people.

**D. Make notes about your partner's movie and describe it to the rest of the class.**

*My partner's movie:* ______________________________

*Story:* ______________________________

______________________________

# Practice

## 1 Dialog

**A. Listen to the recording and put the missing words into the dialog.** Track 36

| weekend | comes | really | shame |
|---|---|---|---|
| booked | about | prefer | movies |

**Steven:** Are you busy this ________________, Marie?

**Marie:** Actually, I do have plans on Saturday. I'm going to the movies.

**Steven:** Oh, ____________? What are you going to see? Anything fun?

**Marie:** I'm gonna see ***Je t'aime, Mon Amour***. It's a **romance** film.

**Steven:** Oh, I heard ________ that. The **French** one, right? I heard good things.

**Marie:** Would you like to join me? I haven't ___________ the tickets yet.

**Steven:** Well, I'm not really a fan of **romance** movies. I ________ **action** and **comedy**.

**Marie:** That's a ________. I like all kinds of ___________, actually, not just romance.

**Steven:** When the next ***Captain Adventure*** movie ________ out, would you like to see it?

**Marie:** **Guy Francis** is in that, right? He's so handsome.

**B. Look at the bolded words in the dialog above. With a partner, think of some new information to replace these words.**

**C. Practice the dialog using the new information.**

## 2 Picture Description

**Listen and choose the statement that best describes what you see in the picture.** Track 40

1.

Ⓐ Ⓑ Ⓒ Ⓓ

2.

Ⓐ Ⓑ Ⓒ Ⓓ

## 3 Unscramble

**Unscramble the sentences below.**

1. the movie / made me / This is / cry. / that
   → ______________________________

2. who was / The actor / that movie / my favorite. / in / is
   → ______________________________

3. watched last / The program / night / was sad. / that we
   → ______________________________

4. which make / He likes / him laugh. / movies
   → ______________________________

5. used to go / The theater / has closed / that we / down. / to
   → ______________________________

## Note Taking

| Main Points | Detail |
| --- | --- |
| | |
| | |
| | |
| | |
| | |
| | |

| Summary |
| --- |
| |
| |
| |
| |
| |
| |

## Brainstorming

# Journal/Activity Writing

# UNIT 11 Telling Stories

Warm-Up

Talk about something memorable that happened to you recently.

**Talking About:**
Things that have happened to us

## 1 Model Dialog

**Listen and practice the dialog with a partner.** Track 41

**Josh:** Did you have a good weekend, Cheryl? You went to the beach, right?

**Cheryl:** Well, I was going to go with my sisters. But the weather was awful.

**Josh:** Yeah, it was. Did you do something else instead?

**Cheryl:** Yes, we had traveled all the way to the beach, so we went to the Sea View Arcade.

**Josh:** That's a shopping center, isn't it?

**Cheryl:** Yep, it's huge. We spent ages looking at the sales, and we each got a manicure.

**Josh:** That sounds nice. My weekend was terrible.

**Cheryl:** Oh, really? How so?

**Josh:** I got stood up on a blind date. Then I was late to work on Sunday, and I got fired!

**Cheryl:** Oh, no! Did your alarm clock not go off?

**Josh:** Yeah, I think the batteries died. Well, I'm off to look for a new job!

### Speaking Success!

There are certain common **idioms** and **phrasal verbs** that are used to talk about everyday occurrences.

**To stand (someone) up**
= *to miss an appointment*

**To get fired**
= *to be removed from one's job*

**To go off** = *to start ringing*

## 2 Vocabulary

**A. Listen to the pronunciation of these regular simple past verbs. Write each verb in the correct column according to its pronunciation.** Track 42

| | | | | | |
|---|---|---|---|---|---|
| visited | promised | moved | played | performed | laughed |
| walked | brushed | showed | cried | graduated | liked |

| /d/ | /t/ | /id/ |
|---|---|---|
| ______ | ______ | ______ |
| ______ | ______ | ______ |
| ______ | ______ | ______ |
| ______ | ______ | ______ |
| ______ | ______ | ______ |

**B. Work with a partner. Make sentences with these words.**

*I **promised** to see my grandmother on the weekend, so I **visited** her on Sunday.*

## 3 Essential Expressions

**Look at the sentences below. Fill in the blanks with the following words.**

| | | | |
|---|---|---|---|
| promised | graduated | walked | visited |
| showed | played | liked | spend |

1. Last week I ________________ my cousins in Alabama.
2. It was a dark night, so I ________________ home with my friend to feel safer.
3. Her younger sister ________________ from college last month.
4. They ________________ each other that they would always be friends.
5. They had to ________________ the weekend packing up boxes before they moved.
6. Rachel ________________ this house much more than her old one.
7. He ________________ them the present he had bought for his wife.
8. The three of them ________________ video games all day long.

## 4 Listening

**A.** **Listen as Lewis talks about some things he did yesterday. Check "True or "False" for each item.** Track 43

| | True | False |
|---|---|---|
| 1. He got up before 9:00. | | |
| 2. He ate breakfast. | | |
| 3. He checked his email. | | |
| 4. He did laundry. | | |
| 5. He washed his car. | | |
| 6. He worked out at the gym. | | |
| 7. He played basketball. | | |
| 8. He went shopping. | | |
| 9. He went to a movie. | | |
| 10. He went to bed before midnight. | | |

**B.** **Turn the above statements into *Yes/No* questions. Ask a partner what Lewis did yesterday.**

Did he get up before 9:00? *Yes, he did.* (True) / *No, he didn't.* (False)

**C.** **Think of some more *Yes/No* questions. Ask your partner about the past.**

Did you watch television yesterday? *Yes, I did. I watched a soap opera.*

## 5 Story Time

A. Work in a group. Look at the two stories below. In your groups, take turns adding new sentences to the stories. Make sure to use the simple past.

It was a hot, humid night. A man walked into a restaurant. When he sat down, he saw a beautiful woman sitting across the room . . .

Ruby just finished working twelve hours. She walked to the station and got on a jam-packed train . . .

B. Look at the pictures below. Work with a partner. Choose at least two of the following pictures. Make up a story using these images and the words provided.

take
bath
ring

1

2

play
see
miss

play
lightning
start

3

4

swim
see
shark

ride
stranger
ask

5

6
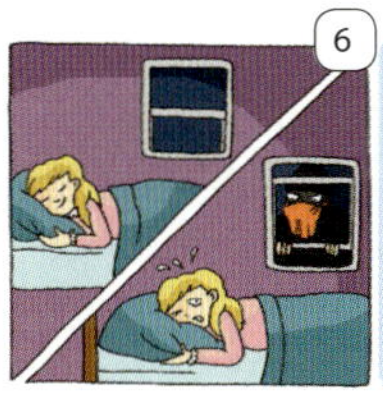

sleep
burglar
come

C. With your partner, tell your story to the group.

## 6 Partner-Up

**A.** **Mr. Parker is very angry. Yesterday his students behaved very badly during class! Write the simple past forms of these verbs.**

| | | | | | |
|---|---|---|---|---|---|
| 1. talk | ________ | 2. sleep | ________ | 3. read | ________ |
| 4. listen | ________ | 5. play | ________ | 6. chew | ________ |
| 7. put on | ________ | 8. copy | ________ | 9. blow | ________ |

**B.** **Work with a partner. Look at the image and talk about what each person did wrong. Use the simple past.**

What did this girl do wrong? *She talked on the phone.*

**C.** **Now do the same, using the past progressive tense. Look at page 11 if you need a reminder.**

What was he doing? *He was sleeping on his desk.*

**D.** **Did you ever do anything bad at school? Discuss in a group.**

*I was mostly a very good student in middle school, but one day I . . .*

# Integrated Learning

## 1 Comprehension

**A. Read the story below. Fill in the blanks with the simple past form of these verbs.**

have see be go

One night, a bald man 1______ at a party. He 2______ a handsome young man. The man 3______ lots of hair and 4______ very popular with women.

The bald man 5______ sad because when he 6______ young he 7______ lots of hair and 8______ lots of girlfriends, too.

The next morning, he 9______ to a toupee shop to buy a toupee.

**B. Complete the story, using your own imagination. Draw pictures and describe what is happening in each panel. Make sure to use the simple past.**

**C. Work in a group. Present your story.**

# Practice

## 1 Dialog

**A. Listen to the recording and put the missing words into the dialog.** Track 41

| ages | weekend | sisters | Sunday |
|---|---|---|---|
| died | awful | traveled | terrible |

**Jacob:** Did you have a good ____________, Cheryl? You went to **the beach**, right?

**Cheryl:** Well, I was going to go with my _________. But the weather was __________.

**Jacob:** Yeah, it was. Did you do something else instead?

**Cheryl:** Yes, we had ______________ all the way to **the beach**, so we went to the **Sea View Arcade**.

**Jacob:** That's a **shopping center**, isn't it?

**Cheryl:** Yep, it's huge. We spent ________ looking at the **sales**, and we each got a **manicure**.

**Jacob:** That sounds nice. My weekend was ________________.

**Cheryl:** Oh, really? How so?

**Jacob:** I got **stood up on a blind date**. Then I was late to work on ______________, and I got fired!

**Cheryl:** Oh, no! Did your alarm clock not go off?

**Jacob:** Yeah, I think the batteries ________. Well, I'm off to look for a new job!

**B. Look at the bolded words in the dialog above. With a partner, think of some new information to replace these words.**

**C. Practice the dialog using the new information.**

## 2 Picture Description

**Listen and choose the statement that best describes what you see in the picture.** Track 44

1.

Ⓐ Ⓑ Ⓒ Ⓓ

2.

Ⓐ Ⓑ Ⓒ Ⓓ

## 3 Unscramble

**Unscramble the sentences below.**

1. I bought / for my / Yesterday / a new / mother. / sewing machine
   → ______________________________

2. how to / My sister / fix a / taught me / broken fusebox.
   → ______________________________

3. feel sick / too much / I / last night. / as I / this morning, / drank
   → ______________________________

4. sang beautifully / Melissa / school performance / last night. / in the
   → ______________________________

5. think about / and he / I spoke / said he / would / to the / it. / principal,
   → ______________________________

## Note Taking

| Main Points | Detail |
| --- | --- |
| | |
| | |
| | |
| | |
| | |
| | |

| Summary |
| --- |
| |
| |
| |
| |
| |
| |

## Brainstorming

# Journal/Activity Writing

# UNIT 12 Travel

**Talking About:**
Travel and vacations

**Warm-Up**

Imagine someone is traveling to your country for a vacation. Which three sights would you recommend they visit?

## 1 Model Dialog

**Listen and practice the dialog with a partner.** Track 45

James: Are you going anywhere for your summer vacation?

Lauren: Yeah, I've just booked my tickets, actually. I'm going to Vietnam.

James: Vietnam! Wow, that's great! I've never been there, but I heard it's amazing.

Lauren: Yeah, I'm so excited. I'm going for two weeks. Are you going anywhere?

James: I'm going to France to visit my parents.

Lauren: Oh, that's amazing! I went to Paris a long time ago.

James: Yeah, they moved there a few years ago. They live in the south, in Nice.

Lauren: Can you bring me back something? They're little cakes called madeleines.

James: Yes, I know them. They're so delicious. I'll try to bring some, if I don't eat them all!

Lauren: Thank you very much. Have a great vacation!

### Speaking Success!

***So*** and ***very*** are often used interchangeably in informal speech, where only ***very*** would be used in writing.

I'm **so** excited.
= *I'm **very** excited.*
Thank you **so** much.
= *Thank you **very** much.*
They're **so** delicious.
= *They're **very** delicious.*

## 2 Vocabulary

**A.** **Write the correct travel word next to each definition.**

bargain   be careful   pickpocket   taxi fare   sunscreen   currency   suitcase   tap water

1. ________________ - a container for travel clothes and necessities
2. ________________ - payment for a cab trip
3. ________________ - water from a faucet
4. ________________ - the kind of money used in a certain country
5. ________________ - lotion to protect you from the harmful rays of the sun
6. ________________ - to pay attention to your safety
7. ________________ - someone who steals from your pockets
8. ________________ - buying something at a good price

**B.** **Work with a partner. Make sentences using the above words.**

*What **currency** do people use in Turkey?*

## 3 Essential Expressions

**Look at the sentences below. Fill in the blanks with the following words.**

| royal palace | resort | postcard | statue | scenic harbor |
|---|---|---|---|---|
| heavy traffic | fountain | souvenirs | carry-on luggage | airport |

1. This ________________ is so expensive because all the rooms have an ocean view.
2. Thank you for mailing me that beautiful ________________ of Hong Kong.
3. I hope my ________________ will fit in the storage bin above my seat in the plane.
4. The historic ________________ that we saw in the park looked like a king or a general.
5. We enjoyed watching the sailboats going in and out of the ________________.
6. It will be faster to take the subway due to the ________________ on the streets right now.
7. The last king who lived in the ________________ died about fifty years ago.
8. We saw some children playing in the water in the big ________________.
9. You can buy lots of delicious food and many kinds of ________________ at the street market.
10. The only way to get to the tropical island is by boat since there is no ________________ on it.

# 4 Listening

**A.** **Look at the picture. What do you know about this place? Have you been there? Would you like to go?**

**B.** **Listen to Michelle talk about an interesting vacation she has been on. Complete the questions.** Track 46

1. How was your ________?
2. ________ did you ________?
3. How long ________ you go ________?
4. ________ did you go with?
5. What ________ you do ________?
6. Where did you ________?
7. What ________ of food did you ________?
8. What ________ did you buy?
9. How ________ did the ________ cost?
10. What ________ ________ like best about ________ ________?

**C.** **Listen again. Write Michelle's responses to the above questions.**

1. ____________________
2. ____________________
3. ____________________
4. ____________________
5. ____________________
6. ____________________
7. ____________________
8. ____________________
9. ____________________
10. ____________________

**D.** **Work in a group. Talk about Michelle's trip and give your opinions.**

*Michelle seemed to have a great time. I am jealous, as I have never been to America . . .*

## 5 Survey

**A.** **Ask the following questions to three classmates. Write their responses. First, write one more question.**

| | Name ______ | Name ______ | Name ______ |
|---|---|---|---|
| Have you ever been to another country? | | | |
| Which countries have you been to? | | | |
| What is the most interesting place you have visited? | | | |
| What is the worst place you have ever been to? | | | |
| What problems have you experienced while traveling? | | | |
| What is your best memory on vacation? | | | |
| Have you ever been sunburned? | | | |
| What is the best meal you have eaten while on vacation? | | | |
| Have you ever traveled alone? Would you like to? | | | |
| Which place would you most like to travel to? Why? | | | |
| Would you consider living and working in another country? | | | |
| Is there any place in the world that you would not like to visit? Why not? | | | |
| ______________________________ | | | |

**B.** **Work in a group. Talk about the most interesting answers that you heard.**

*Terry said that the best meal he ate on vacation was mussels in Belgium, but his worst memory is that they made him sick!*

**C.** **As a class, ask your teacher the above questions.**

## 6 Partner-Up

**A.** Listen to the dialog and perform both roles with a partner. Track 47

**Agent:** **Wonder Airlines**. May I help you?

**Caller:** Yes, I'd like to reconfirm my flight to **Vancouver**.

**Agent:** OK. May I have your name, please?

**Caller:** My name's **Marcus Brennan**.

**Agent:** One moment, please . . . all right, Mr. **Brennan**, you are confirmed on Flight **WA827**, leaving at **10:05 a.m.** on **Sunday, January 2nd**.

**Caller:** It leaves at **10:05**?

**Agent:** That's correct. Please check-in two hours before departure.

**Caller:** OK. Thank you.

**Agent:** You're welcome. Thank you for choosing **Wonder Airlines**. Goodbye.

**Caller:** Goodbye.

**B.** With your partner, practice the dialog with the following details.

- Sky High
- Johannesburg
- Brandon Glover
- SH670
- 2:00 p.m.
- Friday, May 17th

- Air World
- Edinburgh
- Hakim Jones
- WW99
- 11:55 p.m.
- Monday, February 28th

- Asia Express
- Shanghai
- Jeffrey Leech
- SH670
- 2:00 p.m.
- Tuesday, August 14th

**C.** Practice the dialog again, using your own ideas for flight details.

# Integrated Learning

## 1 Comprehension

**A. Work in a group. Read the passage below. Take turns reading it aloud.**

### Sunshine Beach Resort - Guest Review

This hotel is both good and bad. First, the good: it is in a wonderful location. I walked right out of my room and straight onto the beach. The rooms are big and the beds are comfy, and the breakfast is delicious. Now, the bad: the staff! The staff here are very rude, and not at all helpful. I was locked out of my room, and they charged me $5 to open the door! I hadn't even lost my key! The lunch and dinner at the restaurant are very expensive, but not very good. All in all, I would recommend a different hotel in a similar location.

*** out of ***** stars*

**B. Read again. Write "T" (true) or "F" (false) next to the statements.**

1. This hotel is called Sunshine Beach Hotel. ______
2. The rooms are big and the beds are comfy. ______
3. They charged $50 to open the door. ______
4. The reviewer recommends this hotel. ______
5. The breakfast is delicious. ______
6. The reviewer lost his/her key. ______

**C. Look at the words below. Work in your group. Give each problem a number from 1-8, depending on how badly it would affect your trip.**

| | |
|---|---|
| ____ Flights are delayed | ____ Lost luggage |
| ____ Wallet is stolen | ____ Bad weather all vacation |
| ____ No food on the plane | ____ Loud guests in the hotel |
| ____ Get food poisoning | ____ Lost tickets |

1 ◀ Least Affect Trip ——— 5 ——— Most Affect Trip ▶ 8

# Practice

## 1 Dialog

**A.** **Listen to the recording and put the missing words into the dialog.** Track 45

| amazing | few | booked | vacation |
|---|---|---|---|
| something | bring | anywhere | excited |

**James:** Are you going anywhere for your summer ________________?

**Lauren:** Yeah, I've just ________ my tickets, actually. I'm going to **Vietnam**.

**James:** **Vietnam**! Wow, that's great! I've never been there, but I heard it's amazing.

**Lauren:** Yeah, I'm so ________. I'm going for **two weeks**. Are you going ___________?

**James:** I'm going to **France** to visit my parents.

**Lauren:** Oh, that's _________________! I went to **Paris** a long time ago.

**James:** Yeah, they moved there a ________ years ago. They live in the south, in **Nice**.

**Lauren:** Can you ________ me back ______________? They're little **cakes** called **madeleines**.

**James:** Yes, I know them. They're so delicious. I'll try to bring some, if I don't eat them all!

**Lauren:** Thank you very much. Have a great vacation!

**B.** **Look at the bolded words in the dialog above. With a partner, think of some new information to replace these words.**

**C.** **Practice the dialog using the new information.**

## 2 Picture Description

**Listen and choose the statement that best describes what you see in the picture.** Track 48

1.

Ⓐ Ⓑ Ⓒ Ⓓ

2.

Ⓐ Ⓑ Ⓒ Ⓓ

## 3 Unscramble

**Unscramble the sentences below.**

1. have been / We / twice already. / back
   → ______________________________

2. spent a / have / by the / We / lot of time / pool.
   → ______________________________

3. I have / been / never / there.
   → ______________________________

4. has traveled / He / Asia. / all over
   → ______________________________

5. stayed in / five times. / We have / this hotel
   → ______________________________

## Note Taking

| Main Points | Detail |
|---|---|
| | |
| | |
| | |
| | |
| | |
| | |

| Summary |
|---|
| |
| |
| |
| |
| |
| |

## Brainstorming

# Journal/Activity Writing

# Appendix

## UNIT 06 The Weather

**Work with a partner. Partner B looks at this page and partner A looks at page 62. Take turns asking each other questions and write the answers in the spaces.**

### WEATHER AROUND THE WORLD

### Partner B

What's the weather like in HONOLULU in AUGUST?

SYDNEY--MARCH
- It's warm.
- It's often cloudy and rains a lot.
- The high is about 25 and the low is about 17.

HONOLULU—AUGUST
- 
- 
- 

BANGKOK--APRIL
- It's very hot and humid.
- It's usually sunny.
- The high is about 34 and the low is about 27.

SAPPORO—FEBRUARY
- 
- 
- 

LONDON—JULY
- It's usually warm.
- It rains sometimes.
- The high is about 22 and the low is about 11.

HONG KONG—MARCH
- 
- 
- 

AUCKLAND—JUNE
- It's cool.
- It rains a lot.
- The high is about 14 and the low is about 9.

GUAM—JANUARY
- 
- 
- 

SAN FRANCISCO—JULY
- It's usually sunny.
- It's windy sometimes.
- The high is about 18 and the low is about 12.

## UNIT 07 Food

**Mike and Dave eat a lot! Partner B looks at this page and partner A looks at page 72. Ask your partner the questions and then add up the score. Who won?**

### Partner B

| How many . . . | Amount | How many . . . | Amount |
|---|---|---|---|
| 1. . . . bananas did he eat? | | 2. . . . apples did he eat? | |
| 3. . . . eggs did he eat? | | 4. . . . bowls of rice did he eat? | |
| 5. . . . boxes of cookies did he eat? | | 6. . . . slices of pizza did he eat? | |
| 7. . . . pieces of cake did he eat? | | 8. . . . bags of potato chips did he eat? | |
| 9. . . . glasses of milk did he drink? | | 10. . . . bottles of cola did he drink? | |
| 11. . . . cups of coffee did he drink? | | 12. . . . cans of juice did he drink? | |
| | | Mike's score = | |

## UNIT 07 Food

**Work with a partner. Partner B looks below and partner A looks at page 73. Give hints to help your partner guess each word, but do not say the word.**

It's a vegetable. It's long and orange. It tastes sweet— *A carrot!*

Partner B

**What is it?**

It's a kind of fruit. / vegetable. / drink. / snack. / food.

**What shape is it?**

It's round. / oval. / square. / long.

**How big is it?**

It's big. / pretty big. / pretty small. / small.

**What color is it?**

It's green / yellow / brown / pink / red inside. / outside.

**How does it taste?**

It's sweet. / sour. / salty. / bitter.

**What is it like?**

It's light. / heavy. / soft. / hard. / juicy.

## UNIT 09 Shopping

**Work with a partner. Read the sentences on the cards and think of an appropriate response for each. Then follow the instructions on page 93.**

| 5 How much is this? 5 | 5 Could I see that one, please? 5 | 5 Can you help me, please? 5 |
|---|---|---|
| 5 Do you take credit cards? 5 | 5 May I help you? 5 | 5 Where is the restroom? 5 |
| 10 I'd like to return this. 10 | 10 Do you have anything cheaper? 10 | 10 Excuse me, where is the dressing room? 10 |
| 10 It's too tight. 10 | 10 What size are you looking for? 10 | 10 I'm just looking. 10 |

# UNIT 09 Shopping

15
Could you give me a discount?
15

15
It doesn't fit.
15

15
Do you have this in black?
15

15
Would you like to pay by cash or credit card?
15

15
Can I try it on?
15

15
Where can I buy souvenirs?
15

20
Will that be it?
20

20
I'll take this one. Could you (gift-) wrap it, please?
20

20
I don't care for this.
20

20
Where is the information desk in this building?
20

20
We don't accept credit cards.
20

20
Can I get a refund?
20

# Listening Transcripts

## Unit 01 Introductions

### Track 1

**Simon:** Hello, I'm Simon. It's nice to meet you.
**Rachel:** Hi, Simon, my name is Rachel. Glad to meet you. Where are you from?
**Simon:** I'm from Montreal, Canada. I'm here to study history. What about you, Rachel?
**Rachel:** I'm from Canberra, Australia. I study English literature.
**Simon:** That's interesting. When did you come here?
**Rachel:** Two years ago. How about you, Simon?
**Simon:** I came here last month. Do you have any brothers or sisters?
**Rachel:** Yes, I have one sister. She lives with my parents.
**Simon:** I have a sister, too. Oh, my class is about to start! See you later.
**Rachel:** It was nice meeting you, Simon. Have a nice day!

### Track 2

**Man:** What is your name?
**Mary:** My name is Mary Hart.
**Man:** Where are you from?
**Mary:** I'm from Vancouver, Canada.
**Man:** Why did you come to Spain?
**Mary:** I came to teach English . . . and my husband is Spanish.
**Man:** How long have you been here?
**Mary:** I've been here for almost three years.
**Man:** Can you speak Spanish?
**Mary:** Yeah, I can speak some, but not very well.
**Man:** What do you like best about Spain?
**Mary:** I would have to say the food! I really love Spanish food!
**Man:** What do you like the least?
**Mary:** Umm . . . sometimes it's difficult to make good friends.
**Man:** Do you have any children?
**Mary:** No, not yet.
**Man:** Do you have any brothers or sisters?
**Mary:** Yes. I have two brothers and one sister.
**Man:** What do you do in your free time?
**Mary:** Well, I love cooking, and I like eating out, too.
**Man:** Do you have a car?
**Mary:** No, I don't. I pretty much take the train wherever I go.
**Man:** What's your dream for the future?
**Mary:** Hmm . . . someday I'd like to open up my own restaurant.

### Track 3

**Interviewer:** Hi, please sit down.
**Interviewee:** Hello, pleased to meet you.
**Interviewer:** So, could you tell me a little about yourself?
**Interviewee:** Yes, of course. My name is Jack Malden. I'm 21 years old and I live in New York.
**Interviewer:** OK, Jack. Why do you think you are the best person for this job?
**Interviewee:** Well, I am hard-working and motivated.
**Interviewer:** Do you have any work experience?
**Interviewee:** Yes, I was a delivery boy for Pizza Party for two years.
**Interviewer:** Very good. Thank you, Jack. We will be in touch.
**Interviewee:** Thank you. Goodbye!

### Track 4

1. **A.** The woman is the boy's mother.
   **B.** The boy wants to sit next to the woman.
   **C.** The woman has never met the boy before.
   **D.** The boy is giving the woman something.
2. **A.** The woman is introducing the man to her friend.
   **B.** The man is writing down the woman's name.
   **C.** The women are happy to see each other.
   **D.** The parents are walking with their child.

## Unit 02 Family

### Track 5

**Rasheed:** My sister is getting married next week.
**Jen:** Wow, that's great! I don't have any siblings.
**Rasheed:** Oh, really? I have two sisters and a brother.
**Jen:** That's a lot! How old are they?
**Rasheed:** Hmm . . . let me think. My younger sister is 6, and my older sister is 26.
**Jen:** What about your brother? How old is he?
**Rasheed:** He's, uh . . . 18. We're good friends. We often play soccer together.
**Jen:** That sounds nice. I'm an only child.
**Rasheed:** Is it boring at home? My brother is my best friend.
**Jen:** Not at all. My dad comes home early to play video games with me.

### Track 6

1. brother
2. son
3. husband
4. grandfather
5. nephew
6. father

7. uncle
8. wife
9. mother
10. daughter
11. aunt
12. grandmother
13. niece
14. sister

### Track 7

| | |
|---|---|
| **Man:** | Nina, are you married? |
| **Nina:** | Yes! |
| **Man:** | Do you have any children? |
| **Nina:** | No, I don't. |
| **Man:** | Do you have any brothers or sisters? |
| **Nina:** | Yes. I have a sister, Christina, and a brother, Tony—both younger. |
| **Man:** | How old is Tony? |
| **Nina:** | Tony is 17. |
| **Man:** | And how old is Christina? |
| **Nina:** | She's 18 now—she's going to be 19 next month. |
| **Man:** | Stephanie, are you married? |
| **Stephanie:** | No. |
| **Man:** | Do you have any sisters or brothers? |
| **Stephanie:** | Yes, I do. I have three older brothers—Eric, Chris, and Dan. |
| **Man:** | How old are they? |
| **Stephanie:** | Oh, gosh . . . umm . . . OK—Eric is 26, Chris is 24, and Dan is 21. |
| **Man:** | Hilda, are you married? |
| **Hilda:** | Yes. |
| **Man:** | Do you have any children? |
| **Hilda:** | Yes. |
| **Man:** | How many children do you have? |
| **Hilda:** | Five. |
| **Man:** | Five? |
| **Hilda:** | Five. |
| **Man:** | How old are they? |
| **Hilda:** | Uh . . . from 35 to 48. |
| **Man:** | Between . . . |
| **Hilda:** | Between 35 and 48. |
| **Man:** | Could you give me their names and their ages? |
| **Hilda:** | Let's see . . . Ron is 35, Marilyn is 39 . . . Eric is 44, Steven is 45, and Janet is 48. |
| **Man:** | Uh-huh. Wow! Do you have any brothers and sisters? |
| **Hilda:** | Yes, I do. |
| **Man:** | How many? |
| **Hilda:** | I have one living brother. |
| **Man:** | How old is he? |
| **Hilda:** | Uh . . . 76. |

### Track 8

**A.** My dad's name is Robert. He's 68 years old. He lives in Seattle. He's been married for twenty years and has four children. He doesn't work anymore. He's retired, but he used to be a banker.

**B.** My son's name is Jack. He's 19. He lives in Boston, where he's going to college at Harvard. He's still single, but he's getting married next year.

**C.** My sister's name is Laurie. She's 43 years old. She lives with her husband and their daughter in Portland, Oregon. She's a homemaker.

**D.** My niece's name is Rosie. She's 7 years old and is really cute. She lives in Portland and she's in second grade.

**E.** My uncle's name is Darren. He's 60 years old . . . I think. Uh . . . he lives in San Francisco. He's married and has two kids. Uh . . . he's a pilot.

### Track 9

1. **A.** The children are opening a cardboard box.
   **B.** The family is late to the bus station.
   **C.** Each family member is drinking tea.
   **D.** The boy is remembering his first bicycle.
2. **A.** A father is running in the park.
   **B.** The boy is standing next to a large red bag.
   **C.** A father and son are at the beach.
   **D.** The businessman is discussing politics with his nephew.

## Unit 03 Sickness & Health

### Track 10

| | |
|---|---|
| **Ellie:** | Trevor, how are you doing? I haven't seen you for a while. |
| **Trevor:** | Hey, Ellie. Yeah, I've been really sick for the last few days. |
| **Ellie:** | Oh, no, are you OK? I heard there was a virus going around. My mom was sick. |
| **Trevor:** | I guess I had that. I had a headache, a runny nose, and a bad stomach. |
| **Ellie:** | Oh, that's horrible. Are you feeling better now? |
| **Trevor:** | A little bit. I have an exam today, so I had to come in. |
| **Ellie:** | If you feel really sick, just tell your teacher. I'm sure she'll understand. |
| **Trevor:** | She won't. My teacher is Miss Anderton. She hates sick people. |
| **Ellie:** | I know her. She's super-fit, isn't she? She exercises every day. |
| **Trevor:** | And she's never sick. She'll say it's my fault! It's so unfair! |

### Track 11

| | |
|---|---|
| **Woman:** | Do you smoke more than three cigarettes a day? |

**Dean:** Yes. Yes, I do.
**Woman:** Do you get drunk once or more per month?
**Dean:** Yes. Yes, I do.
**Woman:** Do you eat junk food almost every day?
**Dean:** Yes, I do.
**Woman:** Uh–huh. Do you usually get enough sleep?
**Dean:** Yes, I've been getting a lot of sleep recently.
**Woman:** Do you need to lose weight?
**Dean:** I don't think so.
**Woman:** Do you catch a cold more than twice a year?
**Dean:** No.
**Woman:** No?
**Dean:** No, I don't.
**Woman:** Do you have your teeth cleaned once a year?
**Dean:** Yes, I do.
**Woman:** Do you eat fruits and vegetables almost every day?
**Dean:** Yes, I do.
**Woman:** Do you exercise at least three times a week?
**Dean:** Certainly.
**Woman:** Uh-huh. Is work or school stressful for you?
**Dean:** Oh, very much so.
**Woman:** School's stressful?
**Dean:** School is very stressful.

## Track 12

**Man:** How often do you get a cold?
**Hayley:** This year, I've had a cold three times. But, usually only maybe once a year.
**Man:** How often do you get a headache?
**Hayley:** I get a lot of headaches. I get headaches every week.
**Man:** When was the last time that you had the flu?
**Hayley:** The last time I had the flu was last year.
**Man:** Do you have any allergies?
**Hayley:** No, I don't have any allergies.
**Man:** Have you ever been in the hospital?
**Hayley:** Yes, but only one time.
**Man:** Why were you in the hospital?
**Hayley:** I had suspected malaria. I was really sick.
**Man:** OK . . . let's move on. What's something that makes you feel nauseous?
**Hayley:** Certain foods like seafood. Shellfish makes me feel nauseous.
**Man:** What's something that makes you feel dizzy?
**Hayley:** I feel really dizzy when we go really fast in my car.

## Track 13

1. **A.** The boy is looking through a telescope.
   **B.** The doctor is asking the boy questions.
   **C.** The doctor is checking the boy's eyes.
   **D.** They're rearranging the office.
2. **A.** They're using some medical equipment.
   **B.** The doctor is teaching a class.
   **C.** The nurses are standing by.
   **D.** They're putting away medical supplies.

# Unit 04 Hobbies & Interests

## Track 14

**Amy:** Daniel, are you busy this evening?
**Daniel:** Actually, I am. I'm going swimming with my friends.
**Amy:** Cool! Do you go swimming often?
**Daniel:** Uh-huh. I go at least twice a week. It's great exercise.
**Amy:** Oh, that's good. I'm not a very good swimmer. I'm not very athletic.
**Daniel:** What do you like to do in your spare time, then?
**Amy:** I like to stay at home and read a book or watch television.
**Daniel:** I love reading! I try to read every night before I go to sleep.
**Amy:** You do? We should go to the library together sometime.
**Daniel:** Sure, I'd like that. I have to go now. See you later!

## Track 15

**Woman:** Do you like sports?
**David:** Yeah, I love sports.
**Woman:** What sports can you play?
**David:** Well, I can play basketball and many others.
**Woman:** OK . . . what's your favorite sport to play?
**David:** I really like to play basketball.
**Woman:** Basketball. What sports do you dislike?
**David:** I don't like baseball. I can't play it.
**Woman:** Anything else?
**David:** Well, I can do karate, but I don't like it, actually. It's too hard for me.
**Woman:** What else do you like?
**David:** Oh, I really like golf. I don't like soccer. I find it boring.

Woman: OK. You mentioned soccer. Is there any other sport you dislike, or can't play?
David: Well, I've never learned to play tennis, and I don't like swimming. I'm scared of water.
Woman: Anything else?
David: Oh, I know how to play football, but I don't like it! It's so complicated.
Woman: Thanks for your time.

### Track 16

1. Man: Kenta, what are some things you like or dislike?
   Kenta: Things I like or dislike? Well, I really love basketball. That's my favorite sport. And . . . let's see . . . I like playing golf, too, but not as much as basketball. And things I dislike . . . umm . . . I don't like spicy food very much. And I hate . . . hate peas.
2. Man: Jackie, what are some things you like or dislike?
   Jackie: Hmm. Well, I love dancing and . . . I like to go out and sing karaoke, too. I'm not a very good singer. And things I don't like . . . I don't really care for classical music. And I hate rap. I can't stand it!
3. Woman: Matt, what are some things you like or dislike?
   Matt: Oh, I love pizza! I could eat pizza every day and never get tired of it. And . . . I like Japanese food . . . like sushi . . . I eat a lot of sushi. And don't like . . . I don't like my high school history teacher. She's really boring. And I hate history, too!
4. Man: Tina, what are some things you like or dislike?
   Tina: Hmm . . . things I like or don't like . . . umm . . . I love dogs. They're so cute. And I like cats, too. Umm, I don't really like mice, but I hate rats. They're disgusting!

### Track 17

1. A. He already caught a big fish.
   B. The fish has been cooked.
   C. The boy is holding a fishing pole.
   D. He's swimming in the river.
2. A. He is showing his brother how to play the game.
   B. The boys are playing a game on the computer.
   C. The boys are playing a basketball game.
   D. Two friends are watching cartoons.

## Unit 05 Holidays & Dates

### Track 18

Betty: Happy birthday, Michael! It's not much, but I got you this card.
Michael: Wow . . . thanks. Actually, it's not my birthday today.
Betty: It's not? Oh, no! How did I get that wrong?
Michael: It's OK. My birthday is next month, the $14^{th}$.
Betty: February $14^{th}$? Your birthday is on Valentine's Day?
Michael: Yeah, it is. It's a little embarrassing, to be honest.
Betty: Why's that? I love Valentine's Day! It's my absolute favorite holiday.
Michael: Well, my mom always gets me a card with roses on it.
Betty: That's funny. She sounds like fun. Well, do you want this card or not?
Michael: Yeah, I suppose so. It's better than roses again! Thanks, Betty.

### Track 19

1. January $26^{th}$ - Australia Day
2. February $14^{th}$ - Valentine's Day
3. April $1^{st}$ - April Fool's Day
4. April $23^{rd}$ - St. George's Day
5. July $1^{st}$ - Canada Day
6. July $4^{th}$ - Independence Day
7. October $31^{st}$ - Halloween
8. November $11^{th}$ - Remembrance Day or Veterans Day
9. December $25^{th}$ - Christmas

### Track 20

Brad: Hi, Claire. Are you excited for tomorrow?
Claire: Of course, Brad! It's Christmas Day! My favorite day of the year!
Brad: Me, too! What will you do?
Claire: I will open presents with my family.
Brad: Oh, that's great. What about food? Will you have a special meal?
Claire: Usually I eat roast turkey with my close family.
Brad: Sounds good! I love Christmas Day too. Do you know why?
Claire: No, why is that?
Brad: It's the day before my birthday!
Claire: So, your birthday is December $26^{th}$? I hope it's a good one!

### Track 21

1. A. The woman is in front of the fountain.

B. She's looking at the fountain.
C. The water to the fountain is shut off.
D. She is meeting her friend by the fountain.

2. A. They are reading the menu.
B. The man's food is ready.
C. The server is giving them a menu.
D. They're sharing some food.

# Unit 06 The Weather

## Track 22

**Angela:** Oh, are you back from England already? How was it?
**Freddy:** Yes, I got back yesterday. It was great.
**Angela:** I'm glad. What about the weather? I heard their weather is really bad.
**Freddy:** The weather was good, actually. I don't like it when it's too hot.
**Angela:** I love hot weather. The hotter the better! So, did it rain?
**Freddy:** On my last day, yeah. It rained cats and dogs!
**Angela:** Oh, that's too bad. Did you get wet?
**Freddy:** I got soaked to the bone. But it was fun.
**Angela:** Well, that's good! Are you glad to be back again?
**Freddy:** I guess so. But I'm a little under the weather. I think I have a cold.

## Track 23

A. **Woman:** Where did you go last year?
**John:** I went to Shanghai.
**Woman:** China—cool! How long did you stay in Shanghai?
**John:** Eight days.
**Woman:** Eight days . . . OK. What was the weather like in Shanghai?
**John:** Well, I went in August so it was really hot and really humid. But the heat didn't bother me—it was sunny almost every day—not a cloud in the sky.
**Woman:** So, did you have a good time there?
**John:** Yeah, I had a great time!

B. **Woman:** Where did you go this summer?
**John:** I went to Bali.
**Woman:** Bali—wow! I want to go to Bali! How long did you stay there?
**John:** Oh, just for three days . . . not very long.
**Woman:** What was the weather like?
**John:** The weather was horrible! Just my luck—there was a typhoon. It rained every day. And it was very, very windy.
**Woman:** Sounds like you were unlucky! I guess you didn't have a good time, then.
**John:** You know, despite the weather, I did have a good time. I met some really nice people, and I really enjoyed the food.

C. **Woman:** Where did you go?
**John:** Alaska.
**Woman:** Alaska? Ooh—gives me goose bumps! How long did you stay there?
**John:** I was there for a week.
**Woman:** A week? That's enough time to freeze to death! What was the weather like, then?
**John:** Well, it was cold, but not as cold as I thought it would be. The daytime temperature was around 0, and at night it got down to about -20.
**Woman:** Twenty below zero? Yikes! Umm . . . did you have a good time there?
**John:** I sure did! I got to see the northern lights for the first time. It was awesome!

## Track 24

1. A. There are many boats on the water.
B. People are playing in the water together.
C. The lake is very peaceful and quiet.
D. The storm is making the water rough.

2. A. They're brushing snow from their cars.
B. He's building a snowman near the car.
C. Snow is covering the cars.
D. The people are playing in the snow.

# Unit 07 Food

## Track 25

**Jean-Paul:** Melissa, do we have any milk left?
**Melissa:** I think so. There was some this morning when I had my breakfast.
**Jean-Paul:** Hmm. There's none in the fridge. Should I get some?
**Melissa:** Yes, please. Can you get some bananas as well?
**Jean-Paul:** Bananas? Sure, I'll make a shopping list before I go.
**Melissa:** OK, we need yogurt, bread, eggs . . . that's all I can think of.
**Jean-Paul:** Do we have any cola? I really have a craving.
**Melissa:** Cola? That's really bad for your teeth, you know.
**Jean-Paul:** Well, I'll buy some toothpaste, too! By the way, two friends of mine are coming for dinner tonight.
**Melissa:** OK. Then we should pick up some wine, too.

## Track 26

**Woman:** Tony, hi.

**Tony:** Hi.
**Woman:** So, what is your favorite food?
**Tony:** My favorite food? That's tough! I have so many! Let me see . . . pizza, pasta, fried chicken, hamburgers, ice cream . . .
**Woman:** Wow, delicious! Do you think any of them are healthy foods?
**Tony:** Hmm . . . I guess not.
**Woman:** So, you like mainly fast food?
**Tony:** Oh no, not at all. I like healthy foods too. I love bananas, and I really like cabbage, which I know a lot of people really hate.
**Woman:** Well, those are all healthy foods—that's good. What about foods that you don't like?
**Tony:** Don't like? I like most things, but—oh! Broccoli, I absolutely hate broccoli. It's just gross. The taste, the smell, the texture—yuck! Also, it might surprise you, but I don't like chocolate. It's too sweet.
**Woman:** And can you cook anything?
**Tony:** Myself? Oh no, I'm not much of a cook. I can boil an egg actually! That I can do.
**Woman:** One more thing—what would be your perfect meal?
**Tony:** That's easy. My British friend made it for me once. Roast beef with roast potatoes, peas, carrots, and gravy. With Yorkshire puddings. That's kind of like a savory pancake.
**Woman:** That sounds really good.
**Tony:** Oh, it is.

### Track 27

1. **A.** She is doing the dishes.
   **B.** She is taking a bite of the sandwich.
   **C.** She is barbecuing the meat.
   **D.** She is taking a drink of water.
2. **A.** People are bringing the food to the dining room.
   **B.** The lady is serving biscuits to the guests.
   **C.** The wine glass has a napkin in it.
   **D.** There is a lot of food on the table.

## Unit 08 Describing People

### Track 28

**Rafael:** Katie, do you still want to go on that blind date with my friend?
**Katie:** Yeah, I do. I'm a bit nervous, though. What does he look like?
**Rafael:** Well, he's taller than me. And he has shoulder-length hair.
**Katie:** Oh, that sounds nice. What about his eyes?
**Rafael:** His eye color? I don't know. I've never really looked. Maybe blue.
**Katie:** Blue? Wow, that's great. And is he a nice guy?
**Rafael:** He's a great guy. I've known him for a long time.
**Katie:** Well, I hope he's friendly and funny. I like guys who are funny.
**Rafael:** He always makes me laugh. But I laugh at everything!
**Katie:** And one more thing—I hope he's punctual! I hate waiting.

### Track 29

1. My mother is five foot three inches tall. Uh . . . she has light brown hair, but it's starting to go gray. She probably wouldn't want me telling you that. Uh . . . she has dark brown eyes and a round face. And . . . she's fairly skinny. She is very hard-working and polite.
2. Uh . . . my father is five foot seven inches tall. He weighs about 160 pounds. And he has a really big stomach. He also has long grey hair, and it's starting to thin on top. He can be rude, but he is never boring!
3. My best friend is six feet tall. He's got bright red hair, bright green eyes, and a whole lot of freckles. He's really funny, and really lazy sometimes. Like me!
4. My ideal partner is five foot eleven. She has dark brown eyes and dark skin. She is honest and kind. I hope I can find her one day!
5. My favorite actor is Robert De Niro. That's D-E-N-I-R-O. He has a mole right above his lips. I think he is very kind and outgoing, but in his movies he often plays quite scary characters!

### Track 30

**Male Student:** Hey, Stacy, how was class today?
**Female Student:** Oh, terrible. I had Mr. Wallace. He's so mean.
**Male Student :** Mr. Wallace? I know the name, what does he look like?
**Female Student:** He's quite short, and he has a thick mustache.
**Male Student:** I know him. He always wears a yellow sweater.
**Female Student:** That's him! He always gives us so much homework.
**Male Student:** That's too bad. I just had Mrs. Chigwell.
**Female Student:** Oh. She's great, isn't she?
**Male Student:** Yeah, definitely.

### Track 31

1. **A.** The small dog is jumping on the man.
   **B.** He is kissing his dog.

C. The dog and cat are playing together.
D. He is feeding his pet.

2. A. The woman has long, blond hair.
B. The woman has long, dark hair.
C. The woman's hair is not clean.
D. The woman's jacket is very old.

# Unit 09 Shopping

## Track 32

**Sue:** Wow, I love your sunglasses! Where did you get them?
**Nathan:** Thanks. I got them from a fashion outlet store.
**Sue:** Oh, an outlet store, that's good! Where is it? Were they cheap?
**Nathan:** It's not far from here actually, on 6th Street. They were $50.
**Sue:** $50? Wow, that's good. My last pair of sunglasses cost a lot more!
**Nathan:** Yeah, the fashion outlet has lots of great stuff, and the prices are good, too.
**Sue:** Oh, I'll have to go there soon. I need a new pair of jeans.
**Nathan:** Would you like to go there now? I'm not busy.
**Sue:** Oh, great! Do you want to have coffee first? I need a rest.
**Nathan:** No problem. Could you pay for me? I left my wallet at home!

## Track 33

1. 1,120
2. 1,350
3. 845
4. 1,812
5. 3,300
6. 5,750
7. 1,700
8. 7,500

## Track 34

**Man:** Joanne, you are the owner of Shoes, Shoes, Shoes. Can you tell me a little about your store?
**Joanne:** Yes, I can. It is a new fashion store that will be opening downtown this Friday, October 15th.
**Man:** I'm guessing from the name that you will be selling shoes. Am I correct?
**Joanne:** Haha, good guess. At first it will be just shoes, yes . . . but I think we might sell some unique clothes at a later date.
**Man:** And will these shoes be expensive?
**Joanne:** There will be a large range of prices—something for everyone, really. We'll have shoes for $20, shoes for $200!
**Man:** Well, that's good. Everyday shoes and shoes for special occasions. What about shoes for men?
**Joanne:** Yes, we will have a men's section. And a children's section, too! We want everyone to feel welcome.
**Man:** That sounds great. I think your store will be a great addition to our city's shopping scene.
**Joanne:** Thank you. And for our opening week, we will be having a 20% sale on all shoes! Come on down!
**Man:** I will be there! Shoes, Shoes, Shoes opens on October 15th, everyone! Thank you, Joanne.

## Track 35

1. A. The man is buying some fruit at the store.
B. The man is drinking some juice.
C. The man is walking down the road.
D. The man is putting produce into his cart.

2. A. They're waiting in line at the cash register.
B. The man is helping the woman put on a shoe.
C. The couple are shopping in a shoe store.
D. The man is taking products out of the truck.

# Unit 10 Movies & Television

## Track 36

**Steven:** Are you busy this weekend, Marie?
**Marie:** Actually, I do have plans on Saturday. I'm going to the movies.
**Steven:** Oh, really? What are you going to see? Anything fun?
**Marie:** I'm gonna see *Je t'aime, Mon Amour.* It's a romance film.
**Steven:** Oh, I heard about that. The French one, right? I heard good things.
**Marie:** Would you like to join me? I haven't booked the tickets yet.
**Steven:** Well, I'm not really a fan of romance movies. I prefer action and comedy.
**Marie:** That's a shame. I like all kinds of movies, actually, not just romance.
**Steven:** When the next *Captain Adventure* movie comes out, would you like to see it?
**Marie:** Guy Francis is in that, right? He's so handsome.

## Track 37

**Woman:** Darcy, what kind of movies do you like?
**Darcy:** I like to watch action movies.
**Woman:** Who is your favorite actor or actress?
**Darcy:** Well, it's hard for me to choose one actor

or actress, but I guess that I like Emma Watson.

**Woman:** What's the best movie you've ever seen?

**Darcy:** There was a movie called *The Hurt Locker.* It's a tense movie, but I really enjoyed watching it. That's the best movie I've seen, I suppose.

**Woman:** Have you ever seen the same movie more than once?

**Darcy:** Let's see . . . I saw a movie called *Atonement* a couple of years ago, and I liked it so much, I saw it two more times.

**Woman:** How often do you go to the movies?

**Darcy:** Well, I'd like to go more often than I do, but movies are so expensive nowadays. I usually try to go and see a movie about once or twice a month.

**Woman:** OK, what was the last movie you saw, and how did you like it?

**Darcy:** The last movie I saw was a film called *Inception*.

**Woman:** Was it any good?

**Darcy:** Yeah, it was good, but it was too long. People make movies way too long. I did like the story. It had a lot of things going on.

### Track 38

**Husband:** I'm bored. What's on TV tonight? Is there anything good on?

**Wife:** Let's see . . . how about *Real Life Weddings*?

**Husband:** I'm not crazy about reality TV. What else is on?

**Wife:** Well, we can watch the new season of *Police Force*.

**Husband:** *Police Force*? That sounds good. What kind of show is that?

**Wife:** It's a drama. I've heard that it's very good.

**Husband:** Great, let's watch that. What time is it on?

**Wife:** At 7:30 p.m., after the news.

**Husband:** Perfect! What channel is it on?

**Wife:** Channel 6. That's my favorite channel, actually.

### Track 39

**Man:** So, we're talking about movies. Who's your favorite actor or actress?

**Kalani:** I do like Julia Roberts. I like her and Tom Cruise.

**Man:** So, how often do you go to the movies?

**Kalani:** Uh . . . once or twice a month.

**Man:** Once or twice a month? How often do you rent videos?

**Kalani:** Umm . . . not very often, 'cause I can borrow them from the library.

**Man:** Which movie do you want to see?

**Kalani:** Umm . . . I've been wanting to see *American Beauty* again . . . because it's . . .

**Man:** You saw it once?

**Kalani:** Yeah, I saw it in the theater when it came out. Yeah, I loved it.

### Track 40

1. **A.** The television is not working.
   **B.** The woman enjoys watching movies alone.
   **C.** This person is an actor in a comedy program.
   **D.** He is changing channels.
2. **A.** The store is filled with computers.
   **B.** The televisions are huge.
   **C.** The woman is shopping for DVDs.
   **D.** The DVD is a new release.

## Unit 11 Telling Stories

### Track 41

**Josh:** Did you have a good weekend, Cheryl? You went to the beach, right?

**Cheryl:** Well, I was going to go with my sisters. But the weather was awful.

**Josh:** Yeah, it was. Did you do something else instead?

**Cheryl:** Yes, we had traveled all the way to the beach, so we went to the Sea View Arcade.

**Josh:** That's a shopping center, isn't it?

**Cheryl:** Yep, it's huge. We spent ages looking at the sales, and we each got a manicure.

**Josh:** That sounds nice. My weekend was terrible.

**Cheryl:** Oh, really? How so?

**Josh:** I got stood up on a blind date. Then I was late to work on Sunday, and I got fired!

**Cheryl:** Oh, no! Did your alarm clock not go off?

**Josh:** Yeah, I think the batteries died. Well, I'm off to look for a new job!

### Track 42

**1.** visited **2.** promised
**3.** moved **4.** played
**5.** performed **6.** laughed
**7.** walked **8.** brushed
**9.** showed **10.** cried
**11.** graduated **12.** liked

### Track 43

**Woman:** Did you get up before 9:00 yesterday?

**Lewis:** Yesterday? Yesterday was Sunday. No, I

didn't! I got up at 1:00 in the afternoon.

**Woman:** Did you eat breakfast?
**Lewis:** No . . . I never eat breakfast.
**Woman:** Did you check your email?
**Lewis:** Yep. I always check my email, every day.
**Woman:** Did you do laundry?
**Lewis:** Oh . . . no, I didn't. My mom does my laundry.
**Woman:** Did you wash your car?
**Lewis:** Yes, I did!
**Woman:** Did you work out at the gym?
**Lewis:** Yeah, I was at the gym for over three hours. I had a really good workout.
**Woman:** Did you play basketball?
**Lewis:** No, I didn't. I was too tired after working out at the gym.
**Woman:** Did you go shopping?
**Lewis:** Yes, I did. I bought a birthday present for my girlfriend.
**Woman:** Did you go see a movie?
**Lewis:** No, I didn't.
**Woman:** Did you go to bed before midnight?
**Lewis:** Yes, I did—because I had to get up really early this morning to go to work.

### Track 44

1. A. Strangers are making small talk at a bus stop.
   B. The men are helping the women carry their bags.
   C. Friends are laughing and talking on the street.
   D. The women are assisting the men.
2. A. The sheep are moving ahead of the shepherd.
   B. The sheep are eating grass.
   C. There are a lot of wolves behind the sheep.
   D. The sheep are chasing the dog.

## Unit 12 Travel

### Track 45

**James:** Are you going anywhere for your summer vacation?
**Lauren:** Yeah, I've just booked my tickets, actually. I'm going to Vietnam.
**James:** Vietnam! Wow, that's great! I've never been there, but I heard it's amazing.
**Lauren:** Yeah, I'm so excited. I'm going for two weeks. Are you going anywhere?
**James:** I'm going to France to visit my parents.
**Lauren:** Oh, that's amazing! I went to Paris a long time ago.
**James:** Yeah, they moved there a few years ago. They live in the south, in Nice.
**Lauren:** Can you bring me back something? They're little cakes called madeleines.
**James:** Yes, I know them. They're so delicious. I'll try to bring some, if I don't eat them all!
**Lauren:** Thank you very much. Have a great vacation!

### Track 46

**Man:** How was your vacation?
**Michelle:** It was great. I had a lot of fun.
**Man:** Where did you go?
**Michelle:** I went to Las Vegas.
**Man:** How long did you go for?
**Michelle:** Umm . . . I was there for about two weeks.
**Man:** So who did you go with?
**Michelle:** Umm . . . I went by myself to begin with. I was visiting a friend. And then another friend came over and joined me there.
**Man:** So, what did you do there?
**Michelle:** We didn't gamble because none of us were 21, but . . . just saw the sights.
**Man:** Where did you stay?
**Michelle:** I stayed at my friend's house.
**Man:** What kind of food did you eat?
**Michelle:** We went to a bunch of different restaurants. We went to the Cheesecake Factory and had spaghetti and cheesecake.
**Man:** What souvenirs did you buy?
**Michelle:** I bought gifts to bring home to friends and family.
**Man:** Like, what kinds of gifts?
**Michelle:** I bought candles and stuffed animals.
**Man:** How much did the trip cost?
**Michelle:** Far too much. Umm . . . I think it cost me . . . the plane ticket cost about $400 . . . and altogether maybe about $550.
**Man:** What did you like best about Las Vegas?
**Michelle:** It was nice to see my friend. And . . . all the hotels, all the theme hotels. The best part was at the Bellagio—they had a water show. That was nice.
**Man:** That's cool!

### Track 47

**Agent:** Wonder Airlines. May I help you?
**Caller:** Yes, I'd like to reconfirm my flight to Vancouver.
**Agent:** OK. May I have your name, please?
**Caller:** My name's Marcus Brennan.
**Agent:** One moment, please . . . all right, Mr. Brennan, you are confirmed on Flight WA827, leaving at 10:05 a.m. on Sunday, January 2nd.
**Caller:** It leaves at 10:05?

**Agent:** That's correct. Please check-in two hours before departure.
**Caller:** OK. Thank you.
**Agent:** You're welcome. Thank you for choosing Wonder Airlines. Goodbye.
**Caller:** Goodbye.

### Track 48

1. **A.** The surfer is going into the ocean.
   **B.** The man is getting into the boat.
   **C.** The surfer is sinking in the water.
   **D.** The man is surfing on the Internet.
2. **A.** The fountain has been turned off.
   **B.** The fountain has three parts.
   **C.** The fountain is taller than the building.
   **D.** They are tossing coins into the fountain.

# Memo